MW00636890

Leading Equity-Based MTSS for All Students

From Amy
*To my mother, my father, my brother and sisters,
my daughters—each one beautifully unique.
To BB—Thank you.*

From Dawn
*To my family, husband, and my children,
who might finally have a sense of "what I do."*

Leading Equity-Based MTSS for All Students

Amy McCart
Dawn Miller

Foreword by Wayne Sailor

FOR INFORMATION:

Corwin

A SAGE Companyy

2455 Teller Road

Thousand Oaks, California 91320

(800) 233-9936

www.corwin.com

SAGE Publications Ltd.

1 Oliver's Yard

55 City Road

London EC1Y 1SP

United Kingdom

SAGE Publications India Pvt. Ltd.

B 1/I 1 Mohan Cooperative Industrial Area

Mathura Road, New Delhi 110 044

India

SAGE Publications Asia-Pacific Pte. Ltd.

18 Cross Street #10-10/11/12

China Square Central

Singapore 048423

Program Director: Jessica Allan

Content Development Editor: Lucas Schleicher

Senior Editorial Assistant: Mia Rodriguez

Project Editor: Amy Schroller

Copy Editor: Cate Huisman

Typesetter: Hurix Digital

Proofreader: Caryne Brown

Indexer: Molly Hall

Cover Designer: Rose Storey

Marketing Manager: Deena Meyer

Printed in Canada

Library of Congress Cataloging-in-Publication Data

Names: McCart, Amy, author. | Miller, Dawn (Dawn D.), author.

Title: Leading equity-based MTSS for all students / Amy McCart, Dawn Miller.

Description: Thousand Oaks, California : Corwin, 2020. | Includes bibliographical references.

Identifiers: LCCN 2019030337 | ISBN 9781544372853 (paperback) | ISBN 9781544394077 (epub) | ISBN 9781544394121 (epub) | ISBN 9781544394206 (ebook)

Subjects: LCSH: Educational equalization—United States. | Children with social disabilities—Education—United States. | Youth with social disabilities—United States. | Student assistance programs—United States. | Behavior modification—United States. | Response to intervention (Learning disabled children)—United States.

Classification: LCC LC213.2 .M44 2020 | DDC 379.2/6--dc23

LC record available at https://lccn.loc.gov/2019030337

This book is printed on acid-free paper.

MIX
Paper from
responsible sources
FSC® C103567

21 22 23 10 9 8 7 6 5

CONTENTS

Visit the companion website at
resources.corwin.com/LeadingEquityBasedMTSS
for downloadable resources.

FOREWORD

My former doctoral student, Amy McCart, and I started working together in 2000 on what we considered to be a fresh approach to the wicked problem of inclusion. Most of my professional career, starting in 1970, had been pursuing inclusion of children and youth with extensive support needs, beginning with desegregation efforts, initially with the deinstitutionalization movement. Later, my emphasis shifted to implementation of Public Law 94-142 in California and Hawaii, operating from my first education position at San Francisco State University. As a clinical psychologist, I have always felt a bit like the proverbial fish out of water in special education, particularly since many of the basic assumptions that underpin the profession have never made much sense to me.

Biggest among these is the foundational construct of "disability" and its myriad categories with economically bound resources and restrictions for application. The construct is pejorative ("dis-ability") and deficit-based. As a result, special education and the related field of developmental disabilities are focused on human limitations rather than on strengths and the potential that their students bring to the teaching and learning endeavor.

By the time I started my tenure at The University of Kansas (KU) in 1992, I had come to the conclusion that "you can't get there from here" with respect to inclusion driven from the platform of special education. It was emerging in the period as a wicked problem, meaning a problem that cannot be solved due to the constraints engendered by the assumptions and definitions that constitute how the problem is framed. The core values of a pluralistic democracy mitigate against segregation of people for any reason, and in the case of education, research clearly supports nonsegregated arrangements, yet the creation of highly specialized and encapsulated resources, driven by policy and guided by the disability construct, mitigate against inclusion and provide continuing justification for maintenance and even new construction of segregated educational arrangements.

In 2000, Amy and I along with several of my faculty colleagues at KU decided to try a different approach. We partnered with what was then a very low-performing school in the Kansas City area to see if applying a different frame on how to utilize existing resources and personnel could serve a turnaround function. This work looked at the way space and personnel were utilized at the school, which underwent a complete reconceptualization over the period from 2000 to 2005. All special classes of any type were phased out, and all personnel on the payroll of the school assumed some pedagogical responsibility. Teachers associated with specialized programs such as those for gifted students, English learners, and special education were reassigned to general education classrooms. All students, including those with very extensive support needs, were fully integrated in various grouping arrangements, including, but not restricted to, general education classrooms, in accordance with a complex master schedule. All students were considered to be "general education students," and stress was put on identifying their strengths in progressing within the general curriculum. Our frame had shifted from including *students* (a *place-based* definition of inclusion) to including *resources* (an *equity-based* definition). The result was striking. In 2005, this school became the top-performing elementary school in the Midwest.

On a parallel track in the early 1990s, Dawn Miller and a small group of very committed individuals from five states started a convening in Iowa to put forward an agenda to change the identification of students with disabilities. They sought to use formative evaluation in a cycle of inquiry that was laser-focused on understanding what enabled student learning. This convening, which would later be known as MTSS Innovations, had a commitment to bridging research to practice led for and by the "doers." They were also well connected to other researchers, organizations, and agencies, and had influence in schools, districts, states, and national organizations that created the talk and call to action about these practices in varied and important ways. The focus on finding your kindred spirits within and across states is what connected Amy and Dawn. They shared a recognition of the need to facilitate district- and school-level reading/literacy and behavioral outcomes for students across Kansas, and began doing so in a partnership between Northeast Kansas Education Service Center and KU.

Meanwhile, I decided to return to my home state and try to scale up our successful method from one Kansas City school to the Ravenswood School District in East Palo Alto, California. Similar results were achieved, including the elimination of all separate classes in all of the districts' schools by 2010. Amy and I then engaged in another replication of the framework in the District of Columbia Public Schools and achieved similar results by 2012. This reframing and restructuring of supports for all students became an alternative way to meet student needs. By this time, our reframed approach to inclusion had become a blend of positive behavioral interventions and supports (PBIS), which Amy had been wholly invested in, and response to intervention (RTI), which Dawn had been invested in as a technical assistance provider and district member.

Back on the Kansas front, MTSS had a long path of bold state directors and leaders who made important policy changes that would allow MTSS to thrive, namely, Betty Withers, Carol Dermyer, Mike Remus, Alexa Posny, Bruce Passman, Zoann Torrey, and Colleen Riley. Without these individuals, the innovative work in schools and districts would not have been able to continue. Our treasured colleague, Dawn, was integral in this work, and she made contributions to those conversations at the state level, which led to the state's current nationally recognized model. From there she joined the Shawnee Mission School District and served on a district team to codesign, support, and evaluate an integrated approach to academic and behavioral support, with the addition of an interdependent special education identification and service delivery model based on the MTSS framework.

Based on our work in Kansas City, New Orleans, and Washington, DC, Amy and I applied for and received a $24.5 million grant from the Office of Special Education Programs (OSEP) to become the National Center on Inclusive School Reform. We decided to name it SWIFT, for Schoolwide Integrated Framework for Transformation; see www.swiftschools.org. It was then, in 2012, that I learned the hard way that a seasoned faculty member may have a lot to learn from a former doctoral student, and that there is a time when the former should get out of the way of the latter. We fought the battle of ideas while sipping cappuccinos in an outdoor café on DuPont Circle in DC. My idea of technical assistance provision was to assemble a cadre of highly trained consultants and send them into schools to show teachers and administrators what to do. Amy had a different idea, and one instrumental to a whole new way to provide intensive technical assistance to accomplish the complex transformation in schools embodied in the MTSS framework. Amy's idea was to focus on school districts and state agencies in concert with schools. Her rationale was that unless districts could develop the capacity—defined as knowledge, disposition, and skills—to support the installation and implementation of sustainable MTSS in schools as well as the capacity to scale up the framework to other schools in the district, the effort would likely be lost due to administrator turnover and policy changes. Further, she had the foresight to realize that district capacity was fully yoked to state education agency policy, and so the state agency also needed to develop the capacity to support the local district efforts. Additionally, she was insistent on a strengths approach rather than a deficit-based approach to technical support. Fortunately, I lost the argument in DuPont Circle, and SWIFT Center concluded in 2018 with a highly successful replication, on a much larger scale, of our earlier work.

We established SWIFT Education Center at KU, which Amy and I codirect (with Amy in the lead) and with Dawn Miller as a member of the executive team. We are now engaged in assisting several states; including California, which embarked on an ambitious initiative to install and implement MTSS statewide in its 10,000+ schools; and districts around the country to implement MTSS and to reframe their approach to support for all students focused on equity.

Now, with that bit of history from my very biased perspective, let's turn our attention to their wonderful book. Here, in Amy and Dawn's collective voice, you get the details of how these complex elements of school transformation actually came about. Not only that, but you get the detailed facts of rollout in the context of a highly personal narrative. You will learn how they got to be the visionaries as well as implementors they are, in the context of their personal histories growing up and the lessons learned from raising their own children. Implementers at the district and school levels will find this book to be an essential resource to undertaking the complex task of school restructuring and transformation to a sustainable MTSS.

Practitioners in comprehensive school reform are usually in search of a guide on how to proceed, as opposed to more academic treatises. This concise book will satisfy that need in a highly readable way. You might think of it as a kind of checklist on how to proceed, but with poignant narrative and real-life examples. These two highly skilled researchers and technical assistance providers have "been there, done that" and with huge successes in their wake. You will learn at the outset the nuances of what constitutes MTSS. From there you will follow a step-by-step blueprint of how to proceed, with all of the presently available tools and resources to aid your journey en route. Finally, you will learn how to effectively make decisions on the basis of organizing, processing, and analyzing your data, and taking action on the basis of what it reveals. This is MTSS from A to Z. Enjoy the journey.

—Wayne Sailor, PhD

PREFACE

We wrote this book because we see educators who believe each and every child, especially those who are traditionally marginalized, should be welcomed and valued members of their local schools and be given the support they need to achieve academic and social success—yet they struggle with how to do that. Our shared goal as education professionals is to transform education so that it benefits all students, their families, and ultimately the communities in which they live. For more than 20 years we have had the privilege of pursuing this goal in partnership with schools, districts, and state education agencies throughout the United States. Together with them we devised and honed the practices that ultimately defined our Schoolwide Integrated Framework for Transformation (SWIFT) Education Center's approach to equity-based multi-tiered system of support (MTSS). Now we share these practices with you.

We are keenly aware that MTSS, as a means for transformation, has as much to do with entering into reflection on and acknowledgment of one's mindset about teaching and learning as it does with using the widely accepted essential practices of screening, progress monitoring, data-based decision making, and evidence-based instructional practices. In recent years, the phrase "all means all" took root with many educators, as they saw MTSS as a way to build systems for all students by changing and enhancing school culture. However, understanding the myriad of student learning needs and the capabilities of students who face challenges (e.g., disability, poverty, language differences, giftedness) is a lingering barrier to establishing equitable systems of support. In this book we aim to show how to create equity-based MTSS that makes a lasting impact on each of your students and brings about a culture of schooling that demonstrates high levels of academic, behavioral, and social outcomes. Equity-based MTSS becomes a means to an end: equity-based thinking, doing, and achieving.

Recent research tells us that implementation of equity-based MTSS can have a demonstrated, positive effect on schoolwide academic student outcomes, particularly in schools with high-need populations (Hicks, McCart, & Choi, 2018). Additionally, MTSS schools can dramatically reduce out-of-school suspensions and office discipline referrals (Hicks et al., 2018). Beyond improving academic outcomes and reducing problem behaviors, schools that use the tools and resources offered in this book can expect students with disabilities to participate and learn fully in general education—thereby improving schoolwide outcomes even more. Given the well-documented fact that students of color are more likely to be referred for special education (Kramarczuk Voulgarides, Fergus, & King Thorius, 2017) and are disproportionately suspended from school (Smolkowski, Girvan, McIntosh, Nese, & Horner, 2016), these tools can make a particularly important impact on the lives of students of color.

We believe that MTSS should (1) celebrate and use the strengths of educators within the system; (2) de-silo traditional educational structures; (3) support every single student, regardless of each student's unique challenges; (4) from the outset, provide attention to sustainability of the system; (5) garner strategic involvement of families from the beginning; (6) insist on removing long-standing policy barriers; and (7) create a sense of community and optimism within education.

This book will take you through what you need to implement MTSS within your school or district, tailored to be effective for your student body. To do this, we first set forth a challenge to establish your personal, and then your team's collective, "why" for MTSS. Why is equitable MTSS important for your school or district? Why is it important for students and families? When individuals and leadership teams take time to establish their "why," the work they do is driven with purpose. You will see at the end of each chapter the "why" behind the work of some amazing educators we have met along the way.

Next, we invite you to mix your why-driven collective purpose with a clear MTSS framework organized by evidence-based domains, such as effective administrative leadership, an integrated educational system, strong family and community engagement, and inclusive policies and practices. With your why (purpose) and this what (the framework), you have the makings for a highly effective school.

With this strong foundation in place, we take you into the "how" of the work through a deep dive into a set of simple tools that make "all systems go" for all students and their teachers. We show you how to accomplish transformation by building on the previous hard work, knowledge, passion, and commitment of educators in your community. We provide the tools for you to organize and systematize resources and achieve better outcomes for all students. Finally, we situate use of these tools in a continuous improvement process that teams leverage to strengthen the system over time.

Prefaces of many books offer guidance on how to read the book. Given that you are educators, and this is a book, we figure you got this. ☺ Please feel free to read it any way you like, write in it, and use it in whatever way makes sense for you. We are glad you are reading it and sincerely hope it helps you accomplish important and meaningful things.

Finally, we want you to know that throughout our careers we have continued to hold to a basic equity principle: to ensure each student's strengths are celebrated and needs understood and taught to. To that end we pose a transformation process that helps each school and district understand its strengths and needs, and equips it to build MTSS within its local context. We encourage readers to think holistically about the resources available within a district, school, and community in order to break from traditional silos, departments, and funding systems (e.g., ELL services, Title I, special education, school improvement) and to create equity through their local version of MTSS. This book will help you, your school, and your district be proactive in living up to this high standard without requiring additional resources to support those who are culturally or linguistically diverse; those who are entering a grade level already demonstrating a command of its curricular standards or objectives; those who are at risk of underperforming or dropping out of school because of economic, family, and other cultural forces; and those who need support for any other reason. Our hope is that this book inspires and guides you to establish an equitable and efficient system to support all learners in this new way to "do school."

—Amy McCart, PhD

—Dawn Miller, PhD

ACKNOWLEDGMENTS

To Kari: When words fail us and the everyday deadlines threaten to drown us, there is Kari. To our true colleague who always manages to have a life raft and wisdom that is beyond measure. Thank you for this book; for it would not have happened without you. Most people say that, but you know (like really know) this to be true. A heartfelt thank you.

To Kylie who can take dramatically complicated theoretical concepts and teaching practices and present them in a manner that is stunningly simple, accessible, and approachable with a touch a whimsy. Thank you for your ability to express visually concepts that words cannot.

To our SWIFT colleagues who helped to create a vision of what "could be" in schools and our educators in the field who work every day making that reality.

Last, thank you to Dr. Wayne Sailor. His visionary approach to education has changed the lives of countless students, ourselves included.

PUBLISHER'S ACKNOWLEDGMENTS

Corwin gratefully acknowledges the contributions of the following reviewers:

Sherry Annee
High School Science Teacher
Brebeuf Jesuit Preparatory School
Indianapolis, IN

Debbee Garcia
Middle School Principal
Secrist Middle School
Tucson, AZ

Charlotte LaHaye
Curriculum Coordinator
Schools of the Sacred Heart
Grand Coteau, LA

Chris Hubbuch, EdD
Director of Secondary Education
St. Joseph School District
St. Joseph, MO

Holly Leach
Superintendent
Northshore Christian Academy
Everett, WA

Patricia A. Weaver, PhD
Professor, Educational Leadership
Henderson State University
Arkadelphia, AR

Shelby West
Instructional Coach and Intervention
Lead Teacher
Lucia Mar Unified School District
Pismo Beach, CA

ABOUT THE AUTHORS

Amy McCart, PhD, is an associate research professor with Life Span Institute and has adjunct faculty status in the Department of Special Education at the University of Kansas. She is Coprincipal Investigator for the Equity Leadership in High Need Schools research grant, funded through the U.S. Department of Education Office of Elementary and Secondary Education. The focus of this work is to bring about equity in student outcomes by developing high-quality, effective instructional leaders. Dr. McCart is also Codirector of SWIFT Education Center, established in 2012 at the University of Kansas. SWIFT is a national research and technical assistance center designed to improve outcomes for all students, with emphasis on students of color and those with the most extensive need for support. Dr. McCart leads an amazing team of technical assistance professionals in urban, rural, and high-need schools across the United States. She learned much from her fellow educators in her work on the ground in a number of urban school districts, including the Recovery School District in New Orleans, Louisiana; the Kansas City, Kansas, public schools; and the District of Columbia public schools. Dr. McCart traveled to Africa to support its Ministry of Education, and she continues to work with these educators in supporting all children.

Dawn Miller, PhD, is the associate director of technical assistance at SWIFT Education Center at the University of Kansas. Her early career focused on creating local educational processes that address student needs and support educators and families. This experience evolved into a role in statewide implementation of a problem-solving process and, ultimately, to her work in her home state's multi-tiered system of support (MTSS) program. As part of these efforts, Dr. Miller was on a committee that created state regulatory changes regarding Child Find and eligibility of children for special education services, and she helped to translate these changes into district procedures linked to MTSS. She also had the opportunity to serve as a district team member leading the planning, staff development, implementation, and evaluation of MTSS. Further, Dr. Miller is part of a national network of like-minded individuals and state agencies who share a vision for and systems approach to supporting student success. She is most appreciative of the extraordinary educators with whom she has had the privilege to work in schools, districts, states, and the nation. Together with them, she strives daily to support the notion of "all students—one system."

INTRODUCTION

Equipping You for the Journey to Effective MTSS

Alice laughed, "There's no use trying," she said; "one can't believe impossible things."

"I dare say you haven't had much practice," said the Queen. "When I was younger, I always did it for half an hour a day. Why, sometimes I've believed as many as six impossible things before breakfast."

— LEWIS CARROLL, *ALICE IN WONDERLAND*

The concept of a multi-tiered system of support (MTSS) gained much attention over the last decade. For some, this felt like another wave of innovation, something that would come rushing into their schools and then go away just as quickly. For others, it was a feeling of due appreciation for how beliefs, science, and practices converge into a single system. In fact, the Council of Chief State School Officers (CCSSO), in partnership with the Collaboration for Effective Educator Development, Accountability, and Reform Center (CEEDAR), describe the skill of creating an infrastructure to enable MTSS as a core competency for initial principal licensure (CCSSO & CEEDAR Center, 2015). Further, many state education agencies include MTSS initiatives in Every Student Succeeds Act (ESSA) state plans and in special education State Systemic Improvement Plan (SSIP) plans. (For examples, see www.cde.ca.gov and www.fldoe.org.)

Not surprisingly, we see much optimism with MTSS, because we have watched schools and their districts achieve important student, system, and community outcomes as a result of their MTSS efforts. Part of their success is attributable to their leaders engaging in the process of asking, "What if?" What would happen if leaders in your system (yep, we mean you ☺) start asking, "What if we had a system that truly met the needs of all students?" and "What if we were able to learn from others, organize our instructional supports, and bring them together in a way that creates a place where students, staff, and families thrive?"

Building effective schools is a persistent, fluctuating task that does not allow for much pause in the process. This book is intended to help ease this effort by providing tools to directly facilitate the implementation of an equity-based MTSS and allow you to make nimble, quick adjustments as student needs become clear. We offer descriptions, definitions, stories, and examples; then we pause and suggest some questions for you to take to your team. We encourage you to explore the ideas we share and ask these questions of your district planning team, your school leadership team, or your professional learning community. For many educators, these team conversations begin the shift in thinking that gives way to full-scale implementation and sustainability of MTSS.

WHAT DO WE MEAN BY EQUITY-BASED MTSS?

Equity and *MTSS*. These two terms, now commonplace in education, can be difficult to explain and even more difficult to describe with actionable steps for educators. So, let's start with their separate definitions, and then what they mean when held as one idea. Let us also be transparent that we are constantly challenging ourselves with our current working definition. Big picture, it represents underpinnings of ensuring honor, voice, access, and ultimately ownership, with a heaping handful of humility.

Equity in education demands each and every student in a community be invited, welcomed, and given a sense of belonging in a system of teaching and learning that is fluid, responsive, and dynamic, and that uses all available resources matched to each student's need (Mijares, Montes, Hukkanen, & McCart, 2017). Equity is about opportunity, access, resource allocation, and culture. This translates to a deep examination of often long-held practices and beliefs about who should, who can, and who will succeed within our schools.

When we say *each and every student in a community*, we are referring to equity in terms of opportunity. Equitable opportunities suggest such questions as, "Do we have an environment (physical building, space) that is available for use with all students? A place where each and every student can go that is not separate or isolated based on race, disability, culture, behavior or socio economic status?" Equity asks us to actively look around and see who is missing from our school and why.

When we say *be invited*, we are referring to equity in terms of voice and access. Equitable access, often discussed as part of IDEA for students with disabilities, has long created challenges for educators in understanding how to apply grade-level standards to students with disabilities, particularly those with significant learning needs. Additionally, this facet of equity means access to all necessary resources and supports for students with behavioral or social-emotional needs, but these resources and supports typically are not available to educators in a timely or systematic way. This situation forces many educators to do the best they can with the resources they are personally aware of. Equitable access also includes entrance to the school environment as well as access to the resources within the environment. It can mean offering all stakeholders a voice in the educational process in a meaningful and productive way. For example, can students safely get to this place of opportunity? Do families have opportunities to talk about their children's school, their children, and relevant and meaningful issues at the school, rather than just party themes or end-of-year celebrations.

When we say *system of exceptional teaching and learning that is fluid, responsive, and dynamic, and . . . resources matched to each student's need,* we are referring to equity in terms of resource allocation that presumes every student can learn and grow and achieve. Do we allocate our resources in a way that aligns with that belief? Equitable resource allocation, when applied to school funding formulas, lands in our courts for judges and lawyers to grapple with, leaving educators unsure of the implications their decisions will have on teaching and learning. In our approach to equity, we simply discuss resource allocation as it relates to the supports and resources that are currently available within a school or district, giving rise to the question, "Does every single student have access to all available resources based on their learning needs and no other variable (e.g., label or funding stream)?"

When we say *welcomed and given a sense of belonging,* we are referring to equity as a culture that brings together a multitude of backgrounds and characteristics. We strive to understand and grow these existing cultures and beliefs into an equitable school culture that celebrates the unique contributions of each human being within it. We have a direct focus on understanding race, culture, class, needs, personalities, and how these mix together to create a community. This community is one in which there is a deep sense of belonging on the part of all who enter. No one feels as if school is not a place for them.

When we bring up the topic of equity in our discussions, things get serious really quick. As much as we want this book to be fun and a little lighter to digest than other books about equity, the topic remains quite heavy. This weight is real, because, despite the efforts of many educators, we haven't quite gotten as far as we would like at improving academic, behavioral, and social-emotional learning for all students. Many of us haven't wrestled with, or come to a place of individual understanding about, inequities that still exist in all our systems. So then, we keep trying. We acknowledge where *we* are at, individually and collectively, with the angles of equity (e.g., race, socioeconomic status, disability, behavior). We have to own the issues that are part of our past and those we will make ourselves vulnerable to in the future. We also know we are best served if we commit ourselves to being part of a solution that will achieve an equitable system.

> *Equity in education demands each and every student in a community be invited, welcomed, and given a sense of belonging in a system of exceptional teaching and learning that is fluid, responsive, and dynamic, and that uses all available resources matched to each student's need.*

With this understanding of equity in mind, we challenge you to actively look around and think about this definition in relation to the multitude of children around you.

Have you considered equity for children of color, children who are homeless, children who are head of household? What about foster children, or children who are undocumented? What about children in urban communities and children from rural communities? What about children with disabilities? What about children who are using substances, or have mental health issues or have threatened violence? What about children who are obese or are terminally ill, or medically fragile? What about children who are victims of abuse or experienced other forms of trauma? What about children who are English learners, or who are deaf or have autism? What about indigenous children? What about children who are gifted? Children who have parents in prison? What about children who have poor attendance or have served time in juvenile detention? What about children who want to drop out? What about every child who is sitting on the outside whom we may have missed?

This list of "what about this child" is really at the heart of every equity discussion. Leaders know their schools and know that this is a topic that needs careful consideration. Here is an activity for you to start a thoughtful, safe dialogue about equity with your team.

TAKiNG IT TO THE TEAM

EQUITY

- What is in our school environment for all students?

- What are the indications that all families, students, and staff are invited into, feel welcomed at, and have a sense of belonging in our school? Can you think of instances when someone might not feel this way?

- What are the indications that all families, students, and staff see themselves as part of our school community?

- Do all students have access to the same opportunities?

- Are all students known by several school staff—known in a way that their strengths and needs are understood so that we ensure their needs are addressed?

MY THOUGHTS

MTSS is a comprehensive set of academic, behavioral, and social supports that rely on data to mobilize and coordinate diverse resources for students. The U.S. Department of Education (2014) in *My Brother's Keeper Promising Practices Series* on inclusion, equity and opportunity offers the following description of MTSS:

> A multi-tiered system of support (MTSS) is a framework designed to respond to the needs of all students within a system which integrates, but is not limited to, tiered behavior support (e.g. positive behavioral interventions and supports [PBIS]) and academic (e.g. Response to Intervention—RTI) supports. MTSS is a whole-school, data-driven, prevention-based framework for improving student learning outcomes for all students through a layered continuum of evidence-based practices and systems. (p. 1)

Our definition of MTSS, while similar, reframes the emphasis. We focus on the talents and strengths of the educators in each school to support student needs. We harness and structure those talents in a way that elevates all that we educators have to offer within our schools. It builds on the unique histories and skills of each educator and on his or her rich knowledge of students. It takes history and knowledge and mixes it with a healthy dose of evidence-based practices.

Perhaps more important , equity-based MTSS shifts our thinking and changes the questions we ask from "Who will be included?" to "How will each student be known and included?" We shift from a focus on "What spaces can certain students be placed in?" to "What is this place we call our school? Is this a place in which all students, all educators, and all families feel a sense of connectedness?" Instead of wondering, "Which students can or should we support?" the focus becomes, "What do we need to do to support all students effectively with the full array of all academic, behavioral, and social educational resources?"

Let's put our two terms together to define this new term, that is, equity-based MTSS:

> **Equity-based MTSS** is a complex schooling structure that brings together educator knowledge of context, science, and systems, resulting in positive benefits for *all* students. It is an organizing framework that uses specific data sources to inform decisions coordinating diverse academic, behavioral, and social resources to meet the needs of each and every student in a dynamic and timely fashion.

From time to time throughout this book, we are going to take you on "field trips" that illustrate or provide examples from districts and schools engaged in transformation from business as usual to such equitable teaching and learning systems. Check out some reflections on one community's complex journey to understand equity and MTSS in our first field trip.

FIELD TRIP

DEFINING AND CONNECTING WITH EQUITY

People and systems enter into the work of equity at different times and for different reasons. Sometimes it is a personal "self-check." Sometimes it comes from humility, trying to correct a course of actions that negatively affected groups of students, with or without the actors' knowledge or intent. For others it is an invigorating dialogue that creates a different future for how we understand each other and create different learning places and spaces.

Recently, district and school administrators in a northwestern U.S. community engaged in a conversation that reminded them of their journey to create equity and how that journey connected with their multi-tiered system of support implementation work. The exercise brought the group back to three definitions of equity that shaped their work over the past five years. Their district created the first working definition of equity; the second was from a working relationship with a group that focused on racial equity; and the most recent came as they began partnering with SWIFT Education Center, placing the emphasis on equitable distribution of resources to meet needs of all students. The district's associate superintendent asked colleagues to read these definitions individually and then share an example of how their experience with MTSS might get them closer to the ideals of equity and inclusion for all students they serve in the district. Each definition of equity represented a series of conversations, reflections, and actions that had been part of their collective journey with equity. Weaving the prior work of equity into their current focus on MTSS demonstrated their commitment to creating equitable systems and learning environments. The importance of this work was emphasized by their associate superintendent, who noted, "Our commitment to success for every student is rooted in the ideals of equity and inclusion. We believe that every student can learn, so our district and school improvement efforts must focus on the support each student needs to achieve high levels."

TAKiNG IT TO THE TEAM

MTSS

- Does our school community have a working definition of equity? Of MTSS? Of equity-based MTSS?

- Have we come together with our colleagues to look at all the resources available in our system for students?

- Does this list include resources used by colleagues other than ourselves?

- Do we see an order or pattern in the way the resources are used?

- Are any materials, people, or spaces considered "only for students who..."?

- Have we examined our understanding of equity, MTSS, and how they work together to make a difference for students?

MY THOUGHTS

CONSTRUCTING YOUR MTSS

When you think about transforming your school to be more equitable and systemically support all students—whether it is a high school, middle school, elementary school, or preschool—you can think of the process as being much like constructing a physical building—a house. In the construction process, you start with a plot of land, building materials, tools, knowledgeable builders to use the tools, and a blueprint as a shared guide. The blueprint offers information about key elements of the construction process, for example, where the foundation sits and where the load-bearing walls are. A builder has some leeway in the process to make adjustments, but the information on the blueprint influences the degree to which adjustments can be made. One might build without a blueprint, but one wouldn't quite know what the end product would be.

Constructing equitable MTSS is similar (Figure 0.1). In this case, the school and classrooms serve as the plot of land. The curriculum, instructional materials, and school resources serve as building materials. Computers, pencils, and books are the instructional tools. You, of course, have your educators, who serve as the master builders. The processes we present here are like a blueprint that identifies the core components, both operationally and instructionally, to ensure you can build a successful system that meets the needs of all students.

CONSTRUCTiNG MTSS

Source: SWIFT Education Center (2016).

Figure 0.1. **Constructing MTSS**

Since the early 2000s, behavioral and reading multi-tiered systems have garnered the attention of many schools throughout the United States. As a result, the field of education generally agrees that MTSS is primarily about instruction and support provided for all (or most) students. They agree that some amount of additional, perhaps different, instruction and support is made available to some students. And for a few students, support is intensified to meet their unique needs. That said, we want to make sure we are clear about the fact that instruction and support is to be provided for *all* students—that's equity-based MTSS.

Most districts and states have a vested interest in serving all students. With that commitment comes the necessity to actively seek out how and where students are served. "All" students in many places is still practically "most" students. The "equity" part of our definition of MTSS requires a thoughtful and deep dive into the way in which our educational resources and talents are put to use. With equity-based MTSS, we offer a tiered system of support designed to be fully responsive to all student needs. "Tiers" of support are just that, not a system for labeling students, but a system for organizing and deploying instructional and supportive resources. In equity-based MTSS, no student is permanently, or even temporarily, labeled and served as a "Tier 2 student" or a "Tier 3 student." Rather, instructional resources are available and fluidly distributed to any student on the basis of understood need. In this equitable and inclusive approach to MTSS, all students are served through one system with a continuum of support organized in tiers for immediate use.

In addition to tiers of support, MTSS literature consistently identifies four elements that are considered essential for the system to work. These components are the following:

- teaming structures
- data for decision making
- evidence-based curriculum, instruction, and support materials
- continuous improvement processes

The summary in Figure 0.2 shows the words we like to use to explain the essential elements of MTSS. In short, these components provide the infrastructure for MTSS to be fluid and responsive to student need in a manner that does not require an academic or behavioral crisis to occur before support is provided.

You may already be familiar with other forms of MTSS under different names. Many states, districts, and schools use different terminology for the essential elements that broadly define MTSS (e.g., Tier I, II, III; problem-solving process; primary, secondary, tertiary). We encourage you to use the MTSS vocabulary that is most comfortable for you and your stakeholders. The big idea, in whatever terminology, is that these features (teaming; data; evidence-based practices; and continuous improvement processes) are essential. Our intention is to help you understand what you currently have in relation to these elements and help you to move forward with changes or improvements toward a system of support that is rooted in beliefs about equity and a system that is efficient in meeting the myriad of student needs in your school.

EQUiTY-BASED
Multi-Tiered System of Support

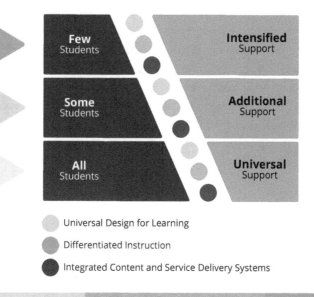

Few Students — Intensified Support

Some Students — Additional Support

All Students — Universal Support

○ Universal Design for Learning

○ Differentiated Instruction

● Integrated Content and Service Delivery Systems

Universal Support

Teams
School Level
Age/Grade/Department Level
Teaching Teams

Data
Universal Screenings
Outcomes Measures
Fidelity Data

Evidence-based Practices
Curriculum
Instruction

Continuous Improvement Process
School and Age/Grade/Dept. Levels
Strengths-based

Additional Support

Expanded Grade & Teaching Teams
Specialists
Parents
Students

Data
Decision Rules
Daily Monitoring
Frequent Progress Monitoring
Fidelity Data

Instruction
Based on Identified Need
Frequency, Duration, &
Timeline Matched to Need
Intended to be Flexible

Continuous Improvement Process
Group and Individual Levels
Strengths-based

Intensified Support

Expanded Grade & Teaching Teams
Specialists
Parents & Students
Community/Agency Service Providers

Data
Decision Rules
Daily Monitoring
Frequent Progress Monitoring
Fidelity Data

Instruction
Based on Identified Need
Frequency, Duration, &
Timeline
Matched to Need
Intended to be Flexible and
Coordinated Across Environments
Continuous Improvement

Process
Individual Level
Strengths-based

Source: SWIFT Education Center (2016).

Figure 0.2. MTSS universal, additional, and intensified support elements

WHAT IS YOUR ANALOGY FOR EQUITY-BASED MTSS?

Each school and district must travel its own path, determining what its MTSS will be in order to meet the needs of its staff, students, families, and community of local stakeholders. Said another way, we equip your team for the journey, but the specific destination is your choice. As an exercise to develop deeper, shared understanding, we suggest that you and your team take a turn at creating your own analogies for equity-based MTSS. It may be that one analogy really sticks, and your team can adopt a shared vocabulary and imagery to communicate while creating (or adapting) your instructional support system to work well in your unique context and culture. Check out an MTSS analogy in the next field trip.

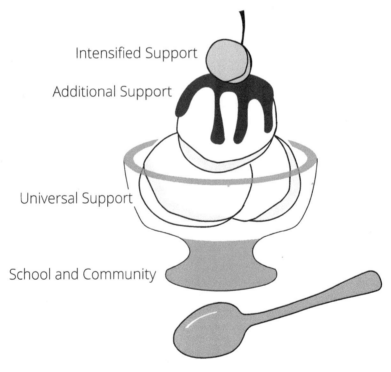

Source: SWIFT Education Center (2016).

Figure 0.3. **MTSS is like an ice cream sundae.**

FIELD TRiP

MTSS ANALOGY

A team from a western state recently described MTSS as like an ice cream sundae. The bowl is the school and community that hold it all together—think of it as a team, with educators, families, and community members working together to serve up education (Figure 0.3).

The ice cream is the universal support, something you want every student to have access to, skills and content that all students need to learn and grow to become ready for full participation in adult life. Good ice cream will have some variation in it to appeal to the different tastes or needs of students, like swirls of fudge, pieces of candy (cookie dough, anyone?) blended right into the base.

For some, the sundae has more fudge sauce over the top, because the swirl was just not enough. (Some people just cannot get enough chocolate.) This second layer may be additional support in the form of extended learning for students who have demonstrated command of the grade-level standards or units of study, or it may be an increased opportunity to put new strategies to use for students who haven't yet demonstrated command.

The third layer on the sundae is a cherry, and maybe some nuts! Not everyone enjoys cherries or nuts, and some may have food allergies that direct their choices. In the same way, not every student will need the same intensified support. This tier of support will vary based on students' individual needs and preferences.

Making an ice cream sundae always involves decisions, just like MTSS. But a great sundae bar and equity-based MTSS are both set up in advance to allow for choices that meet individual tastes or needs, which may not be the same every time. And of course, we want an equitable ice cream sundae bar, which simply means everyone has access to it and to all the possible options on it that meet their interests and needs. Additionally, when enjoying the sundae, they feel a part of the group. In other words, they belong. This analogy (albeit a little lighthearted), offers a way to think about equity-based MTSS as tiered support, available to all with their unique needs in mind.

TAKiNG IT TO THE TEAM

MTSS ANALOGY

- What other analogies help us make sense of equity-based MTSS?

- Sketch some ideas below.

- Examples:

  - Equity-based MTSS is like a coffee house; how?
  - Equity-based MTSS is like a smartphone; how?
  - Equity-based MTSS is like a theme park; how?

MY THOUGHTS

Our experience is that if you are prepared to leverage and build upon your school's and district's existing strengths and local values, as well as to align with your state priorities and academic standards, then you are ready to make MTSS the destination that you need it to be for the long run. This approach to equity-based MTSS can take root in your context and culture, and it can continue to grow and benefit students, staff, and your community. MTSS is here to stay, because it honors what has been and moves us collectively into the future with a full array of resources designed (in advance) to effectively teach our various and sometimes complex student populations.

In short, equity-based MTSS calls upon schools and districts to

- ensure exceptional first, or universal, instruction for all;

- set clear, understandable decision rules for when additional or different forms of instruction and support are warranted;

- schedule and equitably deliver the best available resources when they are needed; and

- monitor and respond to progress data.

WHY DO YOU (YES, YOU) WANT TO "DO" MTSS?

In this book we borrow from our work at SWIFT Education Center to show you how to use a set of tools that are useful for first-time implementation and for continuous improvement. This set of tools helps you orient and engage the whole community in the work of building or improving your MTSS. But be forewarned: Transformation is a dynamic and iterative experience with many entry points depending on local contexts, strengths, and priorities. The process takes many forms and requires quite a bit of trust among all who are involved—especially when questions of equity are at the heart of the matter. Therefore, before we dig into the basics of "how" to implement, we first ask you to travel the path of "why." Yes, that is correct. In order to do this work, you, as an educator, must understand why it is important to invest in a system like this and why you want to do this work. Transformation is not easy, and we are expecting big and mighty things from you. If you read the preface to this book, you know we are talking about changing education—like the whole thing!

So, we ask that you first dive into this question: "Why do I, as an individual, believe that equity-based MTSS is a must for all students?" This is a deep and personal question. Many of us know that we should say that all students can learn and that all students should have access to high-quality education. But deep down we struggle with these principles. Think about a student whose behavior is disrupting the class. Think of the eighth graders who read below a third-grade level. Or a student with significant cognitive challenges. A student who misses countless school days for any number of reasons. Students of color who don't see themselves represented in the curricular materials or don't feel connected or understood. We educators look around our faculty meeting and notice the absence of fellow educators of color. And the list goes on. The "ordinary" demands on educators are high, and now we are suggesting that you include among them the demands of meeting instructional and social needs of all students, including many students with lots of little challenges, or perhaps students with significant challenges—whoever the students in your community are. That is why we dig into the "why" before we go anywhere else.

Within each chapter, one of our field trips will go to "why," with educators who we know are champions of equity-based MTSS. The first one follows here. Then it will be your turn to take it to the team and write out your individual and collective "why."

FIELD TRiP

TERRI'S WHY MTSS

When I was a little girl, I begged my older brother to teach me how to do a backflip on our family's backyard trampoline. He would spend hours spotting me and gently guiding me on a straight path while in midair. As long as my brother was standing there beside me, I was able to do backflip after backflip. However, as soon as he would tell me to try it without being spotted, I would chicken out, terrified that I would fall into the springs. My brother decided (without telling me) that it was time for me to face my fear of falling. One day, while in midair, he nudged me off course, just a little bit, and I, to no surprise, fell into the springs of our trampoline. My feelings were all that were hurt, but I never attempted to do another backflip again. I understand now that my brother never meant to harm me, and only had the best intentions, but his method certainly did not help me reach my goal in any way!

In my 30-year career in education, I have taught in public schools as a special educator and third-grade teacher, and I have been teaching first grade for the past eight years. I have been in many meetings with well-intentioned coworkers, but I walked away feeling frustrated and over-loaded with several strategies and timelines. If the strategies didn't work, I was given more things to try. I often had that feeling again of being "stranded in midair" with no support and no guidance, headed toward a collision. I watched kids move from grade level to grade level, continuing

---

their struggle and getting further behind. My "why" for MTSS is attached to many names and faces who, over the years, I feel our system has failed.

This year is different. My "why" is now attached to a student in my first-grade classroom who is receiving Tier 3 behavior interventions. I am fortunate to be working with a team of educators who understand the MTSS framework. I am no longer expected to figure things out on my own, and I have the support of a team who puts resources into place to help me help *our* student succeed. This student is supported by a variety of individuals in our school, ranging from paraprofessionals to office staff to administrators. Throughout the school year, I have watched this student start letting go of her anger, resentment, and mistrust, and begin to transform into a happy, confident kid who is learning how to take risks. Increasingly she is able to know school as a safe place, where she is accepted and loved. This student, in a way, is doing her own amazing "backflips," and because of MTSS, I will stand alongside my team members and cheer as she lands on her feet.

TAKING IT TO THE TEAM

THE WHY

- Why did you become an educator?

- What keeps you in the profession?

- What do you see with MTSS that would be important to you?

- Do you believe you can and do have a dramatic and lasting impact on students?

- Do you have students for whom you wish the system was different?

- How can MTSS help educators, students, and the system at large?

- Write down your specific "why": Why do I believe in this work?

(Continued)

MY THOUGHTS

If you are facilitating a group in the above team activity, be sure to allow a lot of time for reflection. This is a cornerstone activity that shapes the design of your future together within this framework. Some educators may feel they have students whom they failed or that the system failed (like Terri did). These vulnerable feelings are important for people to share, if they choose. The pressure on educators to be successful with students who may be dramatically complex, and their guilt over the students whose needs they felt they didn't meet, weighs heavily on them and can affect their abilities to be successful educators and transformative leaders. Some may have a family member who inspired them, or a coworker or a child. The "why" of this work cannot be overstated. We often want to rush to "how" and get down to business. Rest assured, articulating our "whys" is an important part of getting down to business.

Between this important reflection on your "why" and an introduction to "how," we would like you to take a few minutes and do one more activity.

TAKiNG IT TO THE TEAM

THE STUDENTS

Make a list of students you have been (or are) concerned about in your school. Go ahead; the list may be long, but this is one of the most important "assignments" we will ask you to do. Think, who are the students who keep you awake at night? These may be students you may, or may not, be directly responsible for. You don't need share the names with anyone else.

Just save the list, because as you continue reading this book, we want you to look at it multiple times. You will notice we repeatedly refer to equity for all students, especially the ones who keep you awake at night. Your list is a vital reference point, a reality check to make sure you are creating a system that ensures all really means all as you embark on this journey.

(Continued)

(Continued)

MY THOUGHTS

HOW TO "DO" MTSS IN YOUR SCHOOL

Now that we have established *what* we mean by equity-based MTSS and *why* we want it in our schools, let's take a sneak peek into the core processes for *how* to do it. We'll share in more detail in the next four chapters.

In Chapter 1 we provide more information about the set of evidence-based practices and implementation processes that set the foundation for MTSS, along with a **resource mapping** process. This process is designed to help teams gain clarity on personnel; facilities; curriculum, instruction, and supports; data sources; and additional resources. It not only creates a shared understanding about available resources, but opens up possibilities for how resources could be used differently to meet identified needs.

In Chapter 2, you will learn to use a **tiered instruction matrix**. This tool allows teams to articulate their plan for decision making about how all students will learn and develop through universal support, along with additional support when needed, and intensified support when warranted.

In Chapter 3, you will learn about reviewing and creating an equity-based **master schedule** for how the school will flexibly use time and personnel, driven by student needs. Educators either love or hate the master schedule! With the way we approach scheduling, this tool becomes central to the MTSS teaching and learning culture. The master schedule becomes a tool to facilitate learning rather than a static description of time and activity allocation.

In Chapter 4, we offer a **resource matching** process. This step brings it all together for each individual student and ensures a system that is responsive, timely, and efficient. We also address how to continuously improve your equity-based MTSS over time, as your context and the world around you continues to change.

Finally, in the Conclusion we will have you check for understanding of the whole big idea (see Figure 0.4 on the following page) with an equity report card.

Okay, so there you go. You just met the processes that will change your life. Well, maybe we are overstating it a bit, but they will change the way you do school. Stick with us. Next you will learn about a foundation that helps to make equity-based MTSS a reality in your school.

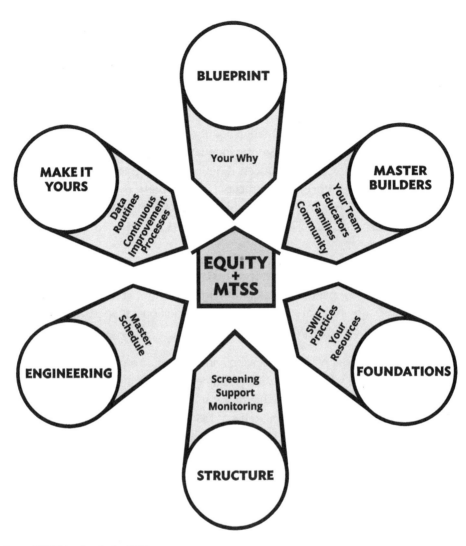

BLUEPRINT

Your Why

MAKE IT
YOURS

Data
Routines
Continuous
Improvement
Processes

MASTER
BUILDERS

Your Team
Educators
Families
Community

EQUiTY
+
MTSS

ENGINEERING

Master
Schedule

SWIFT
Practices
Your
Resources

FOUNDATIONS

Screening
Support
Monitoring

STRUCTURE

Source: SWIFT Education Center (2016).

Figure 0.4. **Guiding metaphor for constructing equity-based MTSS**

1

● ● ●

FOUNDATIONS OF MTSS

> "Will this be easy? No, but it can be done. We are never too old to learn, we are never too meek to lead, and we are never too tired to try again when others' welfare is the goal. This is not the time for fear, rather courage."
>
> —JEFF GRIMES (PERSONAL COMMUNICATION, 2005)

A solid foundation is a must for new construction. It helps ensure that the house is strong, that it cannot be easily destroyed or fall victim to external forces. Laying a good foundation takes time, concentration, and effort on the part of many. Without a good foundation, the time and money invested are wasted.

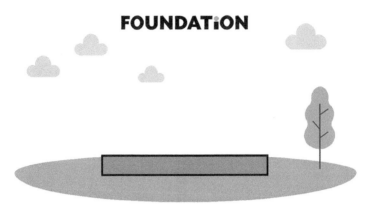

FOUNDATION

Source: SWIFT Education Center (2016).

Figure 1.1. MTSS foundation

The same is true when constructing your equity-based MTSS (Figure 1.1). You want to build a system that is strong and that does not fall prey to the winds of educational initiatives. You want your team to be invested and have the time to focus on strength, stability, and sustainability. When laying your foundation, you want your team to understand the purpose of this work and see the vision of what they will build together in the community. You also want your team to understand why they are investing this initial time and energy and how it will change their future educational practices. Or as we like to say, it will change the way you do school.

Our materials for laying a strong foundation include three elements:

- a framework of evidence-based practices for teaching and learning

- a set of implementation processes grounded in research

- your local resources

We introduce you to the big ideas of the first two, and then teach you how to discover the third through resource mapping.

A FOUNDATIONAL FRAMEWORK FOR TEACHING AND LEARNING

Key to a strong MTSS foundation is the set of interconnected, evidence-based practices shown in Figure 1.2, which when taken together describe a highly effective, equity-driven school. You won't be surprised by them—still, we don't want you to lose sight of them, because they are the forms into which your MTSS foundation is poured, so to speak. They describe the length and width of the foundation—the footprint of the foundation, or the edges to which your system will need to reach.

If you don't build your foundation on the footprint of evidence-based practices, your MTSS will be shaky, at best. The five domains of this framework are shown in Figure 1.2.

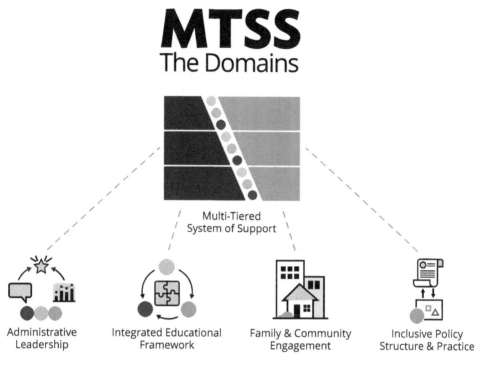

Source: SWIFT Education Center (2016).

Figure 1.2. **Framework for sustainable equity-based MTSS**

We provide more definition to the evidence-based domains and features in the text box that follows. But before you read it, we want to give you a little historical context. When we began our work on this particular framework, we presented all five domains side by side, as equals (Figure 1.3). But then, after analyzing four years of organizational transformation and student outcome data from 64 schools in five states, we changed the structure of our infographic. We found that MTSS was driving the student improvements, with the other domains providing support to implement and sustain the system (Sailor, McCart, & Choi, 2018).

This evidence from the data is why we now visually represent the framework not as five equal domains, but with MTSS at the top and the other four domains holding it up.

You and your team can access some awesome resources for supporting these five domains through guide.swiftschools.org. Be forewarned: You might want to set aside a good chunk of time to check it out. Or better yet, divide and conquer with a "jigsaw" exercise—ask your team members to each investigate a different feature and report back to the team what they found.

DOMAiNS & FEATURES

Administrative Leadership	Integrated Educational Framework	Multi-Tiered System of Support	Family & Community Engagement	Inclusive Policy Structure & Practice
• Strong & Engaged Site Leadership	• Fully Integrated Organizational Structure	• Inclusive Academic Instruction	• Trusting Family Partnerships	• Strong LEA/School Relationships
• Strong Educator Support System	• Strong & Positive School Culture	• Inclusive Behavior Instruction	• Trusting Community Partnerships	• LEA Policy Frameworks

Source: SWIFT Education Center (2016).

Figure 1.3. **MTSS domains and features**

FOUNDATIONAL FRAMEWORK

Strong and Engaged Site Leadership is the foundation for implementing, transforming, and sustaining systems throughout a school. The principal and leadership team empower educators and families to contribute to core school decisions to improve teaching and learning.

Strong Educator Support System provides the structures that enable educators to constantly improve their practices. Instructional supports may include professional learning, instructional coaching, and a supportive, useful evaluation process with a focus on building knowledge and skills.

Inclusive Academic Instruction utilizes schoolwide approaches to promote student learning and high achievement for all students. Schools use powerful instructional strategies, differentiation, universal design for learning, and flexible grouping to support instruction for all students, including

---

those with the most extensive support needs. Academic and behavioral supports are integrated within one multi-tiered system of support.

Inclusive Behavioral Instruction is a proactive approach to teaching social and behavioral skills. Schoolwide supports are designed to be prevention oriented and ensure that social and behavioral supports are addressed at the earliest indication of need with an instructional orientation. Academic and behavioral supports are integrated within one multi-tiered system of support.

Fully Integrated Organizational Structure means full participation in the general education curriculum for all students. All students participate in the general education curriculum instruction and activities with their grade-level peers, and schools embrace ways to redefine roles of para-educators and teaching assistants to support all students.

Strong and Positive School Culture ensures an atmosphere in which all participants know they belong. Particularly, students have equal access to all learning activities, including extracurricular, with appropriate support.

Trusting Family Partnerships contribute to positive student outcomes when family members and school staff have respectful, mutually beneficial relationships with shared responsibility for student learning, when family members have options for meaningful involvement in their children's education and in the life of the school, and when the school responds to family interests and involvement in a culturally sustaining manner.

Trusting Community Partnerships contribute to positive student outcomes when schools work collaboratively with community members, agencies, organizations, businesses, and industry around common goals. Community organizations that represent your student makeup directly participate in school leadership, and enhance school resources.

Strong Local Educational Agency (LEA)/School Relationships promote a shared vision and foster equitable and inclusive teaching and learning. Strong LEA/school relationships use policy to formally organize and integrate initiatives and programs, address and remove barriers to success, and address ways to more effectively use resources.

LEA Policy Framework means that the district or LEA has a formal structure to continually evaluate and rewrite policy in support of quality practices. The LEA uses information from schools to support their schools and ensure staff receive training on relevant research and/or evidence-based practices.

TAKiNG IT TO THE TEAM

FOUNDATIONAL FRAMEWORK

- What examples from our experience show where each of the features described has contributed to positive outcomes for students, families, and staff?

- Which features are strongest in the system where we work?

- Which features raise curiosity or thoughts?

- What features do we still have questions about? (For videos and other explanatory information, check out guide.swiftschools.org.)

MY THOUGHTS

CONTEXTUALIZING THE FRAMEWORK

After learning about this foundational framework, a northwestern district administrative team set about contextualizing it, aligning it with their strategic plan, local culture, and board-adopted values. They rearticulated and reorganized the evidence-based practices with emphasis on elements that reflected these influences, especially their past and ongoing equity work. In the end, their contextualized framework included six domains that were meaningful to them (high-quality academic instruction, student well-being, culture and climate, exceptional staff, family and community engagement, and organizational alignment) with descriptions that explicitly highlighted their belief in and commitment to equity throughout their educational system. Making the framework relevant for their context made it work for them.

FOUNDATIONAL TRANSFORMATION IN ACTION PRACTICES

The second ingredient to mix into the foundation relates to sustainability—the things you do now so that the foundation doesn't crumble or sink later. Think of these practices like the rebars that run inside a concrete foundation. They are installed in the beginning and remain an important part of the structure. You need to do preventive maintenance, but most people don't think much about them after a house is finished.

Sustainable implementation is an Achilles heel of education reform. If you have been around the U.S. public education system for long, you are aware it has had its share of implementation casualties, or seemingly continuous false starts. Time, money, and professional investment have been poured into projects without proper attention to foundational implementation processes. The processes we share with you help make innovations last beyond "shiny and new" and instead grow into "tried and true."

The National Implementation Research Network (NIRN) developed a solid research base for the value and effectiveness of a range of foundational processes for school improvement and reform. (Visit aihub.com for more information.) We applied NIRN's knowledge base to our work and culled out six simple ideas we call transformation in action (TA) practices (Figure 1.4). The TA practices help ensure clarity and consensus for your local ideal for equity-based MTSS, provide a process for evaluating a comprehensive snapshot of outcomes and levels of implementation, and support systematic planning for new ways of working. These practices are briefly described here, with more information and tools available at swiftschools.org/playbook.

TRANSFORMATiON IN ACTION

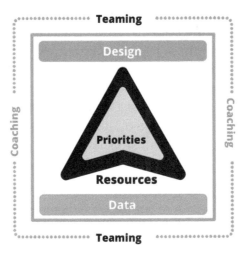

Source: SWIFT Education Center (2016).

Figure 1.4. Transformation in action (TA) practices

FOUNDATIONAL TRANSFORMATION IN ACTION PRACTICES

Teaming defines the roles and communication strategies involved in carrying out whole education system transformation and the supportive TA practices. Teaming helps build capacity to reach more than just one teacher or school. Enlisting teams at the school, district, and state increases the success of implementation and sustainability of the transformation process.

Design is a strengths-based practice that generates a collective agreement about an ideal future education system for all students in a community. Creating a shared design provides coordination and focus to your actions. It also provides an incentive for all involved to collectively work to achieve the design.

The **Data** practice is a process that draws together multiple sources of data to inform decisions. These data sources include student outcome data, measures of the extent to which current practices are implemented, and measures of capacity for sustaining the practices. The process used to analyze data involves prompting shared observations about the data, identifying strengths, and generating opportunities that could leverage strengths in meaningful ways. These data snapshots prompt meaningful conversations about the current state of the system that lead to decisions about priorities for change.

The **Priorities** practice focuses teams on their current stage of implementation for a given educational practice and then identifies steps needed to achieve sustainable use of the practice. This process develops stronger system capacity and enables staff to be comprehensive and intentional in their planning and implementation. This way of planning allows the outcomes of evidence-based practices to be fully realized.

The **Resources** practice is a mapping and matching process that provides a structure to efficiently identify and allocate resources to support implementation efforts. (It is similar to, but not the same as, the resource mapping and matching for ongoing MTSS.) Over time, this process develops stronger system capacity to align and allocate resources for full realization of evidence-based educational practices.

Coaching develops organizational and personnel capacity through use of partnership principles: equality, choice, dialogue, reflection, and reciprocity (Knight, 2014). Coaching may be accompanied by facilitation, which involves direct and intentional involvement with the TA practices in a way that supports acquisition and application of transformative efforts so they can be sustained. Coaching provides a model for developing capacity over time that is durable and sustainable.

We could write reams about how teams engage with our TA practices. (In fact, we have but will spare you the details at this point! Check out McCart, McSheehan, Sailor, Mitchiner, & Quirk, 2016). The important thing to know is that we start from the premise that you have a *team* who actively works to build or strengthen your equity-based MTSS. If you are a team of one (we understand tiny rural schools!), you can still do this work. Your team might not be formally recognized as an MTSS leadership team, but consider yourselves the early visionaries or architects of the work—paving the way for others to be invited in. They'll appreciate the thinking and work you've done to set the stage for MTSS in your school.

TAKING IT TO THE TEAM

TRANSFORMATION IN ACTION PRACTICES

- Who is part of our team, or who would we like to be part of our team?

- What strengths does each individual bring to the table for doing the foundational work of MTSS?

- What do we find intriguing about the TA practices presented here?

- How do we see each of the practices supporting successful implementation of MTSS?

MY THOUGHTS

YOUR LOCAL RESOURCES ARE FOUNDATIONAL TOO

Now that you have the big ideas about the first two parts of the foundation (a framework of evidence-based practices and a set of implementation processes grounded in research), let's consider the third: your local resources.

As we said before, our approach to MTSS focuses on the talents and strengths of the educators in your school, harnesses and structures their talents in a way that elevates all they have to offer, and builds the on their unique histories and skills in order to make equity-based MTSS what is needed to accomplish important educational outcomes for all involved. This way of working differs greatly from old approaches of school reform, where educators were asked to try new practices, often without the necessary support for them to be successful.

Remember, we are laying a foundation for a system of teaching and learning that is fluid, responsive, and dynamic, and that *uses all available resources matched to each student's need.* Because your local resources are foundational for your equity-based MTSS, that's where we suggest you begin—we'll teach you how in the rest of this chapter.

WHAT IS RESOURCE MAPPING AND WHY DO IT?

We have everything we need to get the job done and teach in ways that get our students to work at unprecedented levels.

—JILL JACKSON (2013, P. 53)

We hear it all the time: "I wish we had more _____." Insert people, places, things, time, or whatever you want into this blank, and we bet it will sound familiar to you too. Sure, we always want more of a good thing, but chances are you already have a lot of good things that, when configured in different ways, can get the job done.

We encourage teams who engage in transformation to consider their current reality in terms of available people, places, things, and time they can count on when designing their system. By learning to make the most of resources that we have, we avoid the common error of halting progress because of a perceived lack (or even real lack) of resources. We know how incredibly frustrating it is to be promised new staff or new computers or new curricular materials, only to find out they do not actually become available. Yes, we want to influence these variables—and we encourage continued national, state, and local advocacy to improve the resources available for our students. But we do not want to be paralyzed by uncertainty about whether we will receive more resources in the future. So, our philosophy regarding MTSS installation focuses on the things that are directly in our control. We argue that, while additional resources may allow you to do more or different things, you still have the ability to accomplish amazing things when you give yourselves permission to change the way you think about how you might use what is already available. Don't let the status quo prevent you from improving your system by using what you have right here, right now.

To move into this new way of thinking about resources, we use resource mapping as the first of four for MTSS processes. Resource mapping engages teams in a review of "what is" so that they can make thoughtful and intentional decisions about "what can be done" to meet identified needs. Don't forget, an equitably designed MTSS involves all people, all places, all resources, for all students. If you are going to create an equitable MTSS as one system serving all students through a continuum of support, then your first task is to take stock of all resources that may be part of the one system. Here's how we suggest doing it.

HOW TO DO RESOURCE MAPPING

The idea of taking stock of available resources isn't new. But you may be surprised by what we mean when we say resources, and by how we suggest you use the information you gather (Figure 1.5).

Resource mapping allows recognition of what you have in order to be able to think differently about how you can make the best use of these talents, skills, materials, spaces, et cetera. We like to use the phrase "mine the system" to describe this work of identifying available resources. And we do mean to mine—to dig beneath the surface—to develop a shared understanding that can open up flexibility in team thinking. That said, teams need to know when to stop mining, when continuing to mine no longer adds valuable information to the process and the team gets too deep and loses momentum.

RESOURCE MAPPiNG

Resource & Intention	Task	Example
Personnel		
Increase thinking about all human resources that may be accessed to support student needs.	List all personnel working in the school along with their talents, skills, and interests, regardless of current role and responsibilities	Ms. Hart (5th grade teacher) • book studies • dancing Mr. Choi (Math specialist) • guitar, music • graphic design
Facilities		
Consider all of the space available to the school and how it might be used in new ways to support students.	List all rooms and spaces available in the school building(s) and how it is currently used	Small room next to cafeteria • 1st period; parent resource room Room 105 • M-W-F, 8:30-noon; speech-language therapy
Curriculum, Instruction, & Supports		
Identify all available resources and materials that may be used for academic, behavior, and social-emotional learning instruction.	List curricular material available in the school and how it is currently used	Journeys • supplemental informational text • Instructional framework Read Naturally • fluency, vocabulary
Time Allocations & Requirements		
Identify specific time requirements for core instruction and currently allocated time for providing additional instruction and support.	List the current schedule for delivery of content	ELA block • 120 minutes per day WIN (What I Need) • 45 minutes per day
Data Sources		
Identify all the sources of data that are available for understanding student needs	List all the data sources that teams can access to make instructional and support decisions	• Student Risk Screening Scale • Attendance • FAST Reading
Additional Resources		
Identify any other resources available to support MTSS implementation	List the additional resources available to meet student need across tiers	Boys & Girls Clubs Homework Club

Source: SWIFT Education Center (2016).

Figure 1.5. **Resource mapping**

Sharing the information-gathering load is one way to mine the system without going too deep. There are two ideas we offer for how to gather information for your resource map. The first idea is to establish a Resource Mapping folder on an internal shared drive or Google Drive (Figure 1.6). This folder needs to be something that all the team members can access and edit. Next, for each of the areas listed below, create a nested folder structure for organizing and updating the details of resource mapping over time.

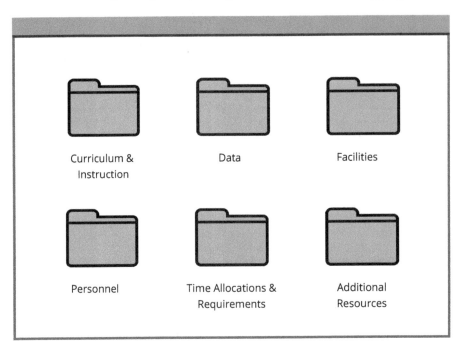

Source: SWIFT Education Center (2016).

Figure 1.6. **Collecting the data together**

The second idea we offer is to gather your team in the library or cafeteria to together create inventories for a few of the categories, such as personnel and facilities. You can do this on sticky notes and wall chart paper visible to the whole team. This approach allows people to grab hold of how the mapping process works through a visual display. Since resource mapping is a new way to think about the resources available to you, we think starting out as whole group is a good idea.

PERSONNEL

Okay, let's start with personnel. Creating a "map" of certified and noncertified personnel allows your team to see the human capabilities in the system. This map starts by simply writing the names of all the staff in, or who serve, your school. Many teams' first instinct is to describe and organize their personnel by formal roles (e.g., first-grade team, science department). This is a good way to make sure you listed everyone, but an inventory by role is just a start. In order to stretch your thinking about human resources, we suggest that you generate a shared understanding of each other by listing talents, skills, and interests. This alternative way of organizing personnel rosters may help you leverage untapped resources to meet student needs. Our experience is that, while mapping personnel begins as a seemingly simple exercise, mining for and acknowledging individual capabilities within each school uncovers new information and creates a bit of freedom in how we view our colleagues and neighbors. This activity is an opportunity to invite discussions of diversity and personal strengths to build a school culture that celebrates not only each and every student but also each and every staff member.

Your school can choose among a range of methods for creating personnel maps. Some schools, in a single work day, collaboratively create "group résumés" using low-tech wall chart paper (Figure 1.7). Other schools take more time and use technology to create a shared, editable document, and their school leadership team invites everyone to add to a bulleted list describing strengths and skills of each individual who serves the school—whether they are school staff, district or regional personnel, and/or parent/community volunteers. Whatever method your team uses, the process will widen your lens to understand the talents, interests, and skills of those who you work with or around, and will recognize the power of your collective educational community.

GRADE 9 MATH PLC

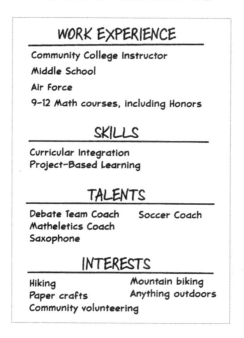

WORK EXPERIENCE

Community College Instructor
Middle School
Air Force
9–12 Math courses, including Honors

SKILLS

Curricular Integration
Project-Based Learning

TALENTS

Debate Team Coach   Soccer Coach
Matheletics Coach
Saxophone

INTERESTS

Hiking   Mountain biking
Paper crafts   Anything outdoors
Community volunteering

Source: SWIFT Education Center (2016).

Figure 1.7. Creating a group résumé

Just imagine how your teams could make stronger matches between instructional support and need when they become aware that a fifth-grade teacher spent years as a kindergarten teacher and is masterful at teaching early literacy skills. Think of the possibilities when your team overtly recognizes contributions a school psychologist can make to the school leadership team because of his penchant for data collection and spreadsheet analyses. Or how a physical education teacher and a student who loves to build things can develop a mentoring relationship as they work together to design an area for a new basketball court outside.

TAKING IT TO THE TEAM

Personnel

- What individual talents, skills, or interests do we have that might be considered differently in our school?

- What is an example of a talent, skill, or interest of a colleague that could be leveraged differently in our school?

- Who works in our school that we realize we don't know much about beyond the job title?

- How can we bring to life the talents beyond traditional roles that educators feel excited about sharing with students?

- Are we considering every staff member in our school? Is every single staff name on our list?

- How might this exercise allow diversity to be understood, celebrated, and leveraged?

MY THOUGHTS

FACILITIES

One of the more interesting tasks teams do for resource mapping is study their use of space and environmental design. We encounter more than a few raised eyebrows when we first ask a team to obtain a blueprint of their building(s) or to sketch out their physical space. However, we know that once a team creates a shared understanding of how their space is currently used and is committed to engage in needs-based instruction and service delivery in that space, they generate innovative ideas that maximize available space for the benefit of all involved.

For example, one team we worked with recognized that a barrier to more flexible use of staff was the designation of four classrooms solely for special education and Title I reading and math instruction (Figure 1.8). Because their plan for achieving equity through MTSS involved more simultaneous small-group instruction, they began to rethink how these four rooms could be used in new ways throughout the school day. Granted, this was not an overnight decision and change. Teachers had desks, computers, and places for things; and they had invested time and money in their classrooms. These were just a few of the issues they had to work through together to make the classrooms available to all students. The team renewed their consensus commitment to use all people, all places, and all resources to meet the needs of all students. They weighed the pros and cons of various space configurations. The team stayed with the process until they were able to ensure a satisfactory course of action that was also respectful and created a positive climate for the educators involved in the change. For this team, the result was established shared learning areas that were flexibly assigned to staff in the master schedule throughout the day.

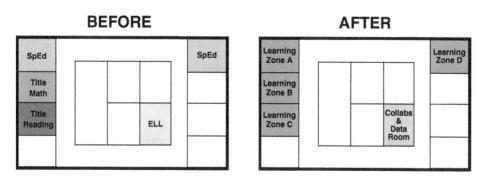

Source: SWIFT Education Center (2016).

Figure 1.8. A facility's before and after plans

Another example of how a building blueprint changed the way a school delivered universal support for good behavior involved community resource officers. The resource officers, who were partners in the MTSS transformation work, recommended having a large blueprint of the school facility and using a colored dot system to indicate where office discipline referrals and incidents occurred. Over time, the team recognized *where* incidents were more likely to occur, which in turn enabled them to generate plausible theories about *why* they occurred and make changes to address the issues. This analysis helped address an important equity issue in the school. Prior to this realization, sixth-grade boys of color were receiving an unusually high number of office discipline referrals. After a look at the environment and the color coding, the team realized this area of the building housed many sixth-grade lockers and was not close to classroom doors, where teachers monitored transitions. This team didn't just assume sixth-grade boys of color have more referrals and that's the way it was. Because they reviewed their facilities, they were able to change the environment by increasing positive adult supervision scattered throughout the halls. This positive change in environment decreased office discipline referrals and made for a more positive school and learning environment. We might add the addition of positive adult supervision included slightly adjusting where existing teachers were positioned, as well as taking advantage of community volunteers. In this school, these community volunteers knew not only each student, but their siblings, parents, and family (one of the beautiful things about a close-knit community).

One more example. A team was studying how their school used space for students who needed additional or intensified supports for English language arts. As the team mapped out student movements through the environment, they became aware that a number of minutes of instructional time were lost due to transitions to small-group instruction. They reasoned that students who receive the most intensified instruction could benefit by staying in the grade-level classroom, while students who were on track could move to alternative spaces for their small-group instruction. The six minutes saved by not transitioning to and from small-group instruction in a different location allowed higher-need students additional practice time to develop more automaticity with the skills the whole class was learning.

As you move into this next activity, help your team to feel safe to try on very creative ideas by assuring them that this is just an exercise for now. Let your team consider the possibility without worrying that they are going to lose their favorite classroom or space. As the discussion continues, people begin to imagine how things could look, and that opens minds to new ideas.

TAKiNG IT TO THE TEAM

FACILITIES

- Are there spaces in our building that are underutilized or overutilized?
- Are there spaces we consider "untouchable" based on their history?

- Has a discussion about a new idea ever been brought to a halt because of a lack of adequate or appropriate space to carry it out?

- Could the physical environment be contributing, positively or negatively, to our current student outcomes?

- Are students moving unnecessarily? Are there other students who need more movement to be successful?

- Have we examined where and when we transition within the building to minimize lost instructional time?

MY THOUGHTS

CURRICULUM, INSTRUCTION, AND SUPPORTS

Perhaps the most daunting task teams face when developing a resource map is taking stock of the vast amount of curricular, instructional, and other resources and supports available across grade levels for academic, behavioral, and social-emotional learning, as well as the specialized instructional areas that are currently used for all students in the school. It may seem like a straightforward thing to do, but be prepared—in our experience your team and their colleagues will have a lot of questions about what goes into this part of a resource map! Just as you do when you map personnel, you want to mine for everything available to meet student needs, but not mine so deep as to lose momentum. This is a good task to break down into smaller chunks, which is what we will do here as well.

For a curriculum and instruction (C&I) map, look for key documents that define the expectations regarding what should be taught, with what materials, when, and how. Many districts create comprehensive documents that make the connections among state standards, grade-level scope and sequence charts, pacing guides, vetted materials, and alignment with an instructional framework with recommendations or guidelines on whole, small, or individual group arrangements. Others provide guidance on part of these C&I elements. Some allow schools to make all the C&I decisions for themselves using the state standards as a guide. The best place to begin this part of resource mapping is with these documents.

The formal documents are just a starting point. Teams should explore the guidance documents together to ensure a consistent and shared understanding of how they pertain to key student groups for whom C&I decisions may have been made by different departments. For example, does the team share an understanding that C&I applies equally to students with disabilities? Students who are learning English as an additional language? Students in an alternate school setting? And so on. This exploration causes our belief structure to meet the mechanics of building our instructional support. If our focus continues to remain on making all resources available to all students, then C&I is one of the most important resources for consideration. We need all curricular and instructional resources and supports to meet the full array of student need based on individual student data.

Some teams quickly realize they need more guidance to get to shared understanding about C&I expectations for different student groups. If your team comes to this realization, you might generate a list of questions for clarification from your district, an intermediate unit, or others who influence students' course of study in your school. Keep in mind, to ask these questions is healthy, often needed, and, in fact, one of the very purposes for resource mapping.

We would be remiss if we didn't remind you and your team to include support materials identified by school psychologists, speech pathologists, Title I staff, those involved at the district level with students learning English as an additional language, occupational and physical therapists, behavioral and social-emotional support staff, and so on. These professionals have amazing resources that may be useful for students beyond those for whom they were originally intended. Often these resources are not diffused across the tiers of support when they can, in fact, be useful for many students.

When mapping these C&I and support materials, your team will want to ensure that they first document those available within the school and then extend their search to their district or intermediate unit. Often curricular materials that were never fully adopted are piled in closets or storage areas—be sure to uncover any gems that may have gathered dust. We do have a caution here: We have noticed as team members who have been in the school or district a while create a resource map, they sometimes slip into "remember when we ...?" and then go in search of those resources. We applaud a team that is thorough in their search, but also recognize and encourage them to be aware of reaching a saturation point when nothing new is emerging from the search, that is, when they are digging too deep.

TAKiNG IT TO THE TEAM

Curriculum and Instruction

- Do we have a comprehensive understanding of resources available to us to address academic, behavioral, and/or social-emotional needs of students?

- Can we think of particular materials used by specific personnel that are not available to all personnel?

- What makes our curricular materials and instructional practices culturally appropriate and relevant? What detracts from cultural appropriateness and relevancy?

- Do we see our students' races and cultures reflected in the materials we have?

- What features of our curricular material do we view as being of high quality? What features are not?

- How are the curricular materials accessible to all learners during the learning process? How are they not?

(Continued)

MY THOUGHTS

TIME ALLOCATIONS AND REQUIREMENTS

This next part of resource mapping is a more straightforward task for teams: to map known time requirements or recommendations and how the available time is used or allocated. The intention is to create a shared understanding of these time factors that influence immediate options for scheduling teaching and learning time. This part of the map feeds into the master scheduling process we describe in Chapter 4.

Demands on time come from multiple sources and vary by content areas, grade levels, and even individual students (e.g., individualized education programs or IEPs). The team should investigate the time demands and make note of the information source for each, so they can test whether it is a requirement (e.g., from law, policy, informal practice) or a recommendation (e.g., from a curriculum developer, from a researcher). For example, your state education agency may provide recommendations for literacy time in elementary school, but your district operates under a board-adopted allocation of minutes that falls short of that standard and poses a challenge to equity-based MTSS implementation. Your team may be able to present new evidence, published subsequent to when the board set this policy, and request that the board review and revise its policy. (We can dream, right?)

Additionally, teams need to be clear on time allocations and requirements pertaining to negotiated agreements for staff. What are the required weekly minutes for planning? Do they differ depending on what the staff do, such as teaching art, music, computer, biology, or time indicated within IEPs? Other details include needing a shared understanding around whether any negotiated agreement distinguishes expectations regarding individual planning versus grade-level planning, and what time is required to consider when teachers share or move between locations (e.g., driving, lunch, breaks).

The challenge we see here for teams is that there are a lot of rules regarding time use. Some of these are "real rules" that must be addressed and built into the schedule. Others are "perceived rules" that have been put into place over time and may have room for negotiation. This process creates an opportunity to think more flexibly about how time is used and improve its use, when possible. For example, when a special education teacher has been serving students in a segregated classroom and the school community desires to move toward general education environments for all students, there are many considerations, including the minutes noted on each IEP and the amount of time the teacher is committed to spending with each student. This transition requires careful planning, communication, and resources use to ensure that student needs are met. And, although the focus of this book is on educators, and not on the family unit, we should always ensure that families are part of the shared vision driving such changes. Their involvement is never more important than when we are trying to change whole educational systems to meet the unique needs of their children. As well intentioned as we are, we can inadvertently fall into the trap of doing things *to* families rather than *with* them.

TAKING IT TO THE TEAM

TIME

- How are decisions made regarding use of time in our school?

- What decisions about time have been our own site decisions? District decisions? State decisions?

- Do we have any perceived time expectations that we might want to consider changing?

- Can we think of creative ideas in which time is allocated differently to meet a need we see in our school?

- Do any of our ideas have implications for families that would suggest reopening a dialogue with them?

MY THOUGHTS

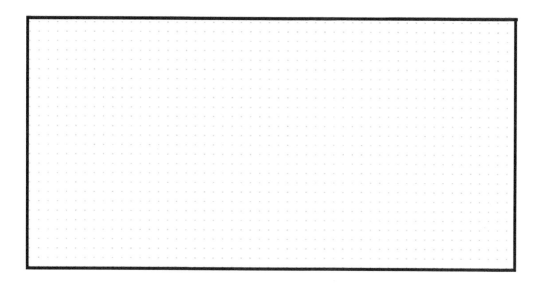

DATA SOURCES

Mapping data sources won't be as arduous as taking stock of curriculum, instruction, and support materials. But mapping data sources will require you to think broadly and create a list that includes data internal to the school as well as data from other parts of the larger system (e.g., district, state, and federal data sources). You want to ensure the list provides a comprehensive snapshot of data that are available to support a variety of decisions related to improving student outcomes (Figure 1.9). Keep in mind that resource mapping is about knowing what is available as a big first step toward articulating how different data sources will, or will not, be used in your equity-based MTSS structure.

School teams are often overwhelmed by the incredible volume of data. The data review of the resource map is often a time when educators can really get their heads around all the sources of information. There was a time when we had too little data, but that is certainly not the case now! We want to look at what we have, so we can begin to determine what is needed and what we can let go.

As you did at other points in this process, you will need time for the team to work through the process, because educators can get a little bit passionate about data. (We love data nerds.) Allow plenty of time, and don't forget to consider:

- Capacity data (e.g., do we have the ability to do this?)

- Implementation data (e.g., are we implementing as intended [with fidelity]?)

- Outcome data (e.g., is this change having the impact we hoped?)

ELEMENTARY DATA SOURCES MAP

	Screening	Diagnostic	Process/Monitoring
Phonological Awareness	**Primary Source** FAST Reading earlyReading English **Supporting Sources** Wonders Weekly Tests/ teacher formatives	**Primary Source** Curriculum-Based Evaluation **Supporting Sources** Wonders Weekly Tests/teacher formatives PAST YOPP-SINGER	**Primary Source** FAST Reading earlyReading English *Indicator selected by need area **Supporting Sources** Wonders Weekly Tests/teacher formatives Intervention Embedded Assessments
Alphabetic Principle	**Primary Source** FAST Reading earlyReading English **Supporting Sources** Wonders Weekly Tests/teacher formatives Quick Phonics Screener	**Primary Source** Curriculum-Based Evaluation DIBELS Deep **Supporting Sources** Wonders Weekly Tests/teacher formatives	**Primary Source** FAST Reading earlyReading English *Indicator selected by need area **Supporting Sources** Wonders Weekly Tests/teacher formatives Intervention Embedded Assessments
Fluency	**Primary Source** FAST Reading CBMreading English **Supporting Sources**	**Primary Source** Curriculum-Based Evaluation DIBELS Deep **Supporting Sources** Multidimentional Fluency Rubric	**Primary Source** FAST Reading CBMreading English **Supporting Sources** Intervention Embedded Assessments
Vocabulary	**Primary Source** *No vocabulary specific subtest can be considered a primary source **Supporting Sources** Wonders Weekly/teacher formatives	**Primary Source** Curriculum-Based Evaluation DIBELS Deep **Supporting Sources** CORE	**Primary Source** **Supporting Sources** Wonders Weekly/Teacher formatives Intervention Embedded Assessments
Comprehension	**Primary Source** FAST Reading COMPefficiency **Supporting Sources** Wonders Weekly Tests/ teacher formatives	**Primary Source** Curriculum-Based Evaluation DIBELS Deep **Supporting Sources** Wonders Weekly Tests/ teacher formatives Comprehension Strategy Rubric	**Primary Source** FAST Reading COMPefficiency **Supporting Sources** Wonders Weekly Tests/ teacher formatives Intervention Embedded Assessments

Source: SWIFT Education Center (2016).

Figure 1.9. **Elementary data sources map**

TAKiNG IT TO THE TEAM

DATA SOURCES

- Do we have a comprehensive understanding of assessment resources available to understand academic, behavioral, and/or social-emotional needs of students?

- Do we have resources that will ensure we understand needs when we think about students who communicate in ways other than verbal responses and/or English?

- Do we have equity for a variety of student groups at the forefront when thinking about our data sources?

MY THOUGHTS

ADDITIONAL RESOURCES

What resources haven't we covered? Don't let the organization system in our book cause you to overlook any gems! Your team can pause and think about any additional resources that might be useful to acknowledge as they pertain to the development of a strong and equitable MTSS. These may include before- and after-school resources, community resources, or other known resources that are worth capturing on your list for future reference. For example, a team we know created a shared Google Document identifying many community agencies they were aware of and a quick list of resources that the team anticipated connecting with in the future. For schools in larger districts, this list may be a set of links to online resources compiled by their local educational agencies.

Another school we were involved with had a growing relationship with leaders of a new church in their neighborhood. The church did not involve the school in its ministries, but it was very interested in serving the school in ways that met student and family needs. Recognizing their access to the church's volunteers allowed the team to think about ways to capitalize on them as an academic resource. Through the school's MTSS, these volunteers provided consistent mentoring and leadership opportunities for students, read to classrooms so that teachers were able to collect data, and were available to promote and support families filling out parent surveys while they waited for their child's parent-teacher conference.

TAKiNG IT TO THE TEAM

ADDITIONAL RESOURCES

- What hasn't been identified as a resource that could be considered by our school team?

- Do we have access to resources that support the unique cultures of the educators and students in our school community?

MY THOUGHTS

Wow, okay we just showered you with a lot of information and activities to set up foundations for your equity-based MTSS. Stand up, stretch your legs a bit, get a glass of water (or a double shot of espresso). We really went deep into the details there. If you need to lift your eyes back up to the big picture, take a field trip into Christi's Why MTSS. Then let's look at how you can structure decision making for flexibly deploying all these resources in a continuum of support for all students.

FIELD TRiP

CHRISTI'S WHY MTSS

As I think about the important work taking place in schools and why I want to be involved in change, I see the faces of specific students. Too many students to name, but students that have never left my mind. The students I had my first year of teaching, the students I worked with as a school principal, and the hundreds of students now in the elementary schools I work with today. The students I felt I somehow did not do enough for, that "we" as a school and system let down, the students I still worry and wonder about.

My first years teaching were in a self-contained special education classroom. No matter how much students progressed and how hard I worked, I quickly realized—this is not going to get them where they need to be. Later, as I taught in general education classrooms, I realized I needed to know more about each one of my students, and I needed to figure out a way to work with each of them on specific areas, but I couldn't fathom how to logistically manage this on my own. As a school principal, I saw students missing class time due to behaviors, behaviors caused not because they were not wanting to do well, but behaviors expected in an environment they had never experienced. At the district level, I see a bigger picture of data shouting something has to change if we want each student to improve.

Why MTSS? For each of those students who did not get what they needed. I know I and we as educators, and as a system, can do better.

2

• • •

STRUCTURING YOUR MTSS

> We can, whenever we choose, successfully teach all students whose schooling is of interest to us. We already know more than we need to do that. Whether or not we do it must finally depend on how we feel about the fact that we haven't so far.
>
> —RON EDMONDS (1979, P. 23)

The process of resource mapping can be an eye-opening endeavor. Teams are amazed to learn of the variety of resources that have been accumulated over time across different grade levels and departments, and this may leave them feeling bogged down rather than wonderfully flexible and dynamic. Never fear! This next tool to use in creating equity through MTSS is called the *tiered instruction matrix* (let's call it the matrix—if that's not too Hollywood for you). This tool brings order to the chaos, establishes a system for easily making decisions as student needs become clearer, and uses the best available resources to get the job done.

We hope each time you read our definition of equity-based MTSS that you consider your why and remember why this hard work is worthwhile.

WHAT IS A TIERED INSTRUCTION MATRIX AND WHY DO IT?

The matrix serves the purpose of organizing and articulating the manner in which the wide range of available resources can be used in a school's MTSS. This book is a blueprint for your team (the master builders) to use as they construct on the plot of land (the school and classrooms), starting with a strong foundation (that is, a framework of evidence-based practices for teaching and learning, a set of implementation processes grounded in research, and your local resources). Now we are ready to think of framing the house—putting up the structure's exterior and load-bearing walls, and maybe the roof, too (Figure 2.1). Visualize an old-fashioned barn raising! Perhaps you can think of the house frame as universal, additional and intensified support; the door frames as universal screening; and the windows as progress monitoring.

STRUCTURE

Source: SWIFT Education Center (2016).

Figure 2.1. **Structure MTSS**

Many schools have universal screening and progress monitoring tools for English language arts (or reading), and are working to get them for mathematics and possibly other subject areas. Remember, universal screeners are used with all students and allow an early snapshot of student academic status. Progress monitoring assessments are also done with all students, but on varying schedules to assess how instruction and support are affecting learning and/or behavior. Newer to this discussion is the need for behavioral and social-emotional screening and progress monitoring tools. These are equally important in understanding the needs of each student and in having timely academic, behavioral, and social instruction matched directly to student needs. If you are looking for some good resources on screeners and monitors, check out the resources at guide.swiftschools.org. Key to a fully functioning matrix is the use of effective universal screeners that are responsive to your unique student population, and clear progress-monitoring tools that are sensitive to the teaching and learning of your educators and students.

Fun fact (well, not really fun, but still a fact): Most educators feel they have way too much data and don't know how to use it efficiently. The matrix we are going to share helps alleviate that problem. Data are used to represent key indicators that help educators create opportunities for all students to get early access to the academic, behavioral, and social-emotional instruction and support they need, when they need it. Too often a time lag between data collection and instructional decision making causes unnecessary delays in student progress, which snowballs over time. (For those of you in warmer climates, we mean a situation in which the results or consequences of an action grow at an increasingly faster rate over time.) With the matrix, we aim to shorten the time lag and take some of the guessing out of the decisions to apply more or different instruction and support mechanisms to meet students' needs with immediacy and efficacy.

The matrix, remember, is the frame. Once in place, it is a structure that can be enhanced and modified but does not required huge overhauls very often. You don't remodel your house every few years, and you won't have to remodel your matrix all that often either. This tool supports decisions regarding instructional strategies and their impact without resulting in decision fatigue. Educators often simply run out of energy as they make so many decisions for so many students across so many areas. This matrix eases that burden (Figure 2.2).

One additional point: Importantly, the matrix serves a bit like a student equity barometer. It allows student need to be at the forefront of the discussion based on data, rather than on other indicators that may inadvertently influence our academic, behavioral, or social-emotional support. Each tier in MTSS includes not just instructional support but also data collection and decision-making features—which is why we refer to tiers that include these parts.

TiERED INSTRUCTION MATRIX

School/District: Grade(s):   Date:

Curricular Area: ☐ Literacy ☐ Mathmatics ☐ Behavior/Social Emotional Learning

Part 1: Universal Support	
What	
When	

Part 2: Universal Screening			
Tools	Who Administers		When Administered
	Additional Support		Intensified Support	
	...to meet benchmark	...when exceeding benchmark	...to meet benchmark	...when exceeding benchmark
Decision Rules	if...then	if...then	if...then	if...then

Part 3: Instruction and Support			
	Who Provides		When Provided
	Additional Support		Intensified Support
Area identified for support	...to meet benchmark	...when exceeding benchmark	options to consider
Skill Area			

Part 4: Progress Monitoring			
Tools	Who Administers		When Administered
	Additional Support		Intensified Support	
	...to meet benchmark	...when exceeding benchmark	...to meet benchmark	...when exceeding benchmark
Decision Rules	if...then	if...then	if...then	if...then

Source: SWIFT Education Center (2016).

Figure 2.2. Tiered instruction matrix

HOW TO CREATE A TIERED INSTRUCTION MATRIX

As a first step before setting up your matrix, we recommend school teams metaphorically clear the foundation of unwanted materials. By this we mean review their accumulated curricular and support materials and protocols (which they can find in their resource mapping files; see Chapter 1). They may decide which resources they want to promote for use and which resources they don't want to promote in their system. We believe that just because we have materials doesn't mean they are suited for the job at hand. Some aren't needed, some aren't wanted any longer, and some were discontinued. Ultimately, through the matrix, your team can articulate

- what is universally available to support all students;

- resources that may be accessed for students who need additional support;

- resources that may be accessed for students who need intensified support;

- how data will be used in the system;

- the instructional/behavioral/social supports that are currently available to meet specific student needs; and

- the manner in which progress will be monitored, including decision rules for flexibly altering support. (Decision rules—stay tuned, these are very important!)

We recommend teams annually review the effectiveness of these broad decisions articulated in the matrix and revise according to data and emerging research (again, not a remodel, just an update). In doing this, you will likely realize some things you want to acquire for your MTSS. Don't let this lack of a resource get in the way of making progress where you can! Keep track of those things for later. Right now, focus on putting up those walls and a roof so your team can "move in." Once in, they can use continuous improvement practices to help inspect and make this place their own.

THE TRIANGLE

Recall our MTSS graphic from the Introduction (reproduced here as Figure 2.3). Sometimes this image is referred to this as the "MTSS triangle." (We know, it is actually a rectangle made of two shapes that are nearly triangles.) If you have been around education in the last decade, you have probably seen a triangle version of tiered support for behavior in positive behavioral interventions and supports (PBIS) and academics in response to intervention (RTI) (Batsche et al., 2005; Sailor, 2009; Sugai, Horner, & Gresham, 2002; University of Texas Center for Reading & Language Arts, 2003, 2004).

EQUiTY-BASED
Multi-Tiered System of Support

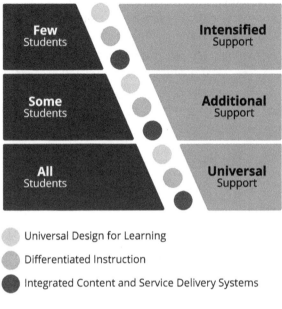

Universal Design for Learning

Differentiated Instruction

Integrated Content and Service Delivery Systems

Source: SWIFT Education Center (2016).

Figure 2.3. MTSS "rectangle"

Hill Walker is credited with the notion of an educational three-tiered model, rooted in the Institute of Medicine's three-tiered public health classification system (Swenson, Horner, Bradley, & Calkins, 2017). The public health model has a broad, first tier of programs that are preventative measures benefiting everyone (e.g., clean water, immunizations). The model's second tier provides support for individuals who need additional care (e.g., daily allergy medication, an "as needed" asthma inhaler, temporary crutches for a broken leg). The third tier serves individuals who need more intensive care temporarily or as support for a chronic condition (e.g., an asthma plan at home and school).

The public health "triangle" or tiered support model made its way over to educational practice through a publication by the University of Texas Center for Reading and Language Arts (2003, 2004) (Figure 2.4). This introduction coincided with new regulations for implementing the 2004 Amendments to the Individuals with Disabilities Education Act. The IDEA regulations included a provision that states must allow, as part of their criteria for determining whether a child has a specific learning disability, the use of a process based on the child's response to scientific research-based interventions. For many of us in the field at the time, we felt the stars had started to align, that is, our values and beliefs about students, education science, and public policy were coming together. It was a beautiful thing! The tiered model proved useful for both behavioral (e.g., PBIS) and academic (e.g., RTI) applications. As we refined our understanding about matching resources to student need, we moved from a single "resource" triangle to complementary triangles matching resources to student needs.

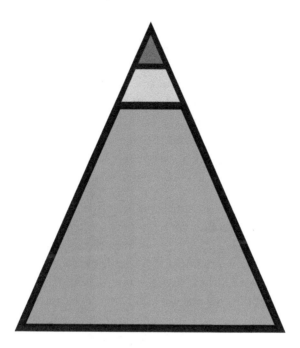

Source: SWIFT Education Center (2016).

Figure 2.4. **Classic triangle of tiered support**

Our mix of triangles, which now forms a rectangle, provides a comprehensive model of evidence for thinking about MTSS with an embedded equity emphasis. On the left-hand side, we emphasize that the system provides teaching and learning for each and every student. (Remember, the "each and every" here is about equity.) As students show their need for more (or less) support, we want to provide it in a way that makes the most efficient use of resources for the students who need it. This aspect of MTSS leads us to the right-hand side of the visual, where we depict the tiers of support that are planned for any student with need. The universal tier is for *all* students—we sometimes refer to this level of support as "best first instruction" across academic, behavioral, and social-emotional domains. When students show a need for more, the visual indicates simply that additional support is provided. And, for a few students, the system needs to more intensely deliver instruction and support to adequately meet their needs.

Are you wondering, "What is that diagonal thing down the middle of the graphic?" This element carries a few messages. First, it indicates that at every level of MTSS, the teaching and learning environment is built with the principles and guidelines of universal design for learning (UDL; CAST, 2018), and functions day-to-day with differentiated instruction. Further, it represents the notion of integration among academic, behavioral, and social-emotional content or competencies, as well as integrated service delivery. Let us explain these integration ideas more fully.

INTEGRATED LEARNING

Integrated academic, behavioral, and social-emotional learning means we don't look at these areas as separate matters. Rather, we seek to understand that student needs are complex and often interconnected. Remember that earlier talk about efficiencies? This is another opportunity to be efficient. For many years we taught ELA, math, and subject matter content with behavior as a secondary focus. As student need shifted, so did our teaching practices. Many of us did not plan, nor did we have the education we needed, to support the complex behavioral needs of some of our students. More recently, student mental health and social needs are requiring another shift in teaching practices. How, then, can we teach all that must be taught within the minutes we have in a day? The answer lies in integrated learning across all tiers.

At the universal tier, an integrated instructional approach requires a direct focus on academic content and behavioral content. Consider the following formula: Start with the academic content to be taught, then select the behavioral or social content to be taught, and combine them. For example, if the academic content is teaching "perimeter and area" and the behavioral focus is "using respectful language," combine the two. As students work in groups, they will practice using respectful language, such as "Jonah, it is your turn to use the rubber band to measure perimeter," and "thank you." This small change puts concurrent focus on the math concept and the social interaction.

An example from a high school context is integration of instruction on the U.S. election process (e.g., how to run for public office, the nomination process for public office) with social learning about how to show respect to others. The students watch YouTube videos of previous candidates making comments about their opponents. They discuss whether the comments were respectful and why. They would then journal about how they would either run for office or help someone run for office (the nomination process) and what they would do to be respectful of the other candidates.

We educators, because of all the demands on our time and attention, often don't think about challenging behavior prior to its occurrence. What integrated learning means is a shift to proactive teaching of appropriate social, emotional, and behavioral skills embedded within academic content formally taught on a daily basis. This integration is a subtle but important shift in this process.

For additional and intensified tiers, we want to use our data to clearly understand the issues. Essentially, we want to find out if we have an academic concern that is related to a behavioral or social-emotional concern; a behavioral or social-emotional concern that springs from academics; or an academic, behavioral, social-emotional concern that is unrelated or interrelated. Think about this example: Jamari needed additional support in reading and needed to learn how to ask for help in an appropriate manner.

His friend, Jules, however, also needed additional support in reading as well as help learning how to resolve conflicts in a nonphysical manner on the playground. Our assessment of the situation was that Jules's playground behavior issues were not related to her reading concerns. While much of the academic support was the same for these two, the behavioral support for Jamari was quite different from the support provided to Jules. For Jamari, it didn't take too long to see that his frustration in reading was related to breaking his pencils and tearing pages in a book. His teacher decided to encourage asking for help anytime he felt he had mild frustration related to a read-aloud request. He was able to do what they called "tap out," which meant he could select a peer to read in his place. They faded this support as he felt more comfortable with reading aloud. Jules received additional reading support without the "tap out" component. For her playground issues, a group practice around "keeping hands to self even on the playground" with a self-monitoring check for Jules did the trick. This use of a menu of supports met both student needs with matched, varied resources.

INTEGRATED SERVICE DELIVERY

Returning to our thinking around Integrated Systems, we don't want to forget a big "must-have" is integrated service delivery. Equity-based MTSS opens up the whole school to think about how to match all resources to all the students' needs, free from educators' individual titles and historical roles. Just as we strive to make sure we don't refer to a student as a Tier 2 or 3 student, we encourage the same fluidity among the adults' roles in the teaching and learning system. Rather than segmented or siloed systems, we build an integrated system of instructional supports and educators rooted within a universally designed system, accessible in multiple ways for the varied needs of all students. That's what that diagonal line means. Too much? We think not.

Ok, now that we have had our history lesson on the use of "the triangle" and an understanding of the components of our rectangle with that ever-important diagonal line, let's jump back into what each part of our matrix represents.

MATRIX PART 1: UNIVERSAL SUPPORT

Commonly held features of the universal tier available to all students include instruction and support through a coherent curriculum designed to address the skills needed for students to be career and college ready upon completion of their schooling process, and a specified pedagogy that frames the instructional practices for delivery and experience. The matrix provides a place for teams to summarize expectations related to this tier. These expectations may include (1) linkages to scope and sequence of standards and skills taught at each grade level or to a schoolwide expectation matrix, (2) expectations for time and instructional grouping arrangements, (3) materials used to support teaching, (4) high-impact instructional practices, and (5) linkages to UDL and planning tools for differentiated instruction.

All that said, in MTSS, all roads lead back to the universal support. If there is one lesson we've learned on our journey with MTSS over the last two decades, it is that if first instruction isn't strong (enough), we have missed the mark. You know the saying, "An ounce of prevention is worth a pound of cure?" All aspects of the universal support deserve the most vigilant attention and nurturing. When asked, educators understandably want support for students who present more academic or behavioral challenges. Yet, if we infuse our universal support with all the support we can muster, the very best of core instruction, high-quality resources, and engaging curriculum, we have fewer students who need extra. (It's true—McIntosh & Goodman [2016] wrote a book about it.)

In Chapter 4 you may notice that the first data review we recommend that you do isn't to see who may need additional support. No, that first data review begins an ongoing conversation about how to strengthen your universal support, your first instruction for all students. The more you make really strong decisions about the universal tier, the more you will be able to use your full complement of resources in innovative ways. For example, if school psychologists don't have to do loads of evaluations, they can redirect their time and expertise to providing support for social-emotional learning among all classrooms. Likewise, reading specialists' time may be freed up to coteach in grade-level classrooms. And the list goes on.

As we move into the details of MTSS, we do not want to lose sight of how our beliefs about equity shape our actions, and remember that equity is a vital outcome of our work. As we do these steps, we must consciously and continually ask ourselves, "Are we making sure we designed our system of support to meet the need of all students?" "Did we design our universal instruction in a manner that will allow every student to engage with it?" And (this is a big one), "Is our design taking into account the cultural considerations of our unique community?" One of our district partners had a relationship with local indigenous peoples, and so they modified their universal tier to embrace and encourage the languages, events, and values that were prevalent in the students' homes. They provided multilingual signage throughout the building, had tribal elders come once a week to teach all students indigenous language, and modified their attendance office communications to reduce mutual misunderstanding around student absences—to name just a few universal modifications. Making such changes to the universal tier is no small task and one of the more fundamental aspects of creating a welcoming culture, a sense of belonging throughout the school.

In the example above, the team considered, "Did we design our universal support in a manner that will allow every student to engage with it?" As another example from a district that had a frequent changes in population based largely on families moving among housing complexes in close proximity to the school, they modified their universal support to include additional support to learn ELA routines and scaffolds as part of the curricular materials. They thought of this support as an ELA boot camp for getting everyone up to speed in a short period of time. If you focus on the core or base level of instruction and make sure it is available and meaningful based on your student population, you are heading in the right direction—which is not only awesome, but effective.

MATRIX PART 2: UNIVERSAL SCREENING

Also part of the universal tier is universal screening. Teams use screening tools with all students for two reasons: (1) to engage in a data review for the purpose of strengthening universal support and (2) to identify students who may need additional support. Note here that the first reason to use universal screening is to strengthen the core instruction. We often think of universal screeners as a way to find out which students need extra, but remember our goal is to always strengthen that universal tier. Bonus points if you remember why. Yes, you are correct, the better our universal tier, the *less we need more.* (Bam! Consider yourself awesome.)

The second reason we use universal screeners is to identify students who "may need" additional support. We put "may need" in quotes, because decision rules help teachers and teams interpret data in reference to an indication of risk. Only after thoughtful consideration and validation of the student's performance do they decide whether to provide additional support resources to meet student need. We really believe that people make decisions about students, not about an assessment or score. This is why we like the term "data-informed" rather than "data-driven."

Much has been written in the literature related to characteristics of universal screening assessments (McIntosh & Goodman, 2016; Pullen & Kennedy, 2019). Broadly, they should have adequate reliability and validity for screening decisions. We are currently aware of reliable screening tools to obtain indications of risk for literacy, math, behavioral, and social-emotional learning at most grade levels—but not all. Sometimes your team may need to make their decisions based on the best level of evidence until a stronger measure emerges. They need to be okay with using their professional judgment in combination with less-reliable assessment information or screening tools until better tools become available. This said, we always need to be on the watch in the literature for advances in this area. Or better yet, stay connected with local college or university and let them help you keep up to date.

In order to ensure that *all* students are accounted for in the universal screening process, your team will want to make a concerted effort to identify any students for whom the universal screening measure is not appropriate. For example, if a student's communication is nonverbal, to screen the student using an oral reading fluency measure would not make sense. In such a case, the team needs to be able to specify a process for obtaining the most valid and reliable indicators available in a particular content area or skill. Likewise, for students who are learning English as an additional language, teams may find it beneficial to understand their literacy or mathematics skills in the student's mastered language in order to make stronger decisions about the most appropriate type of instruction or support needed (e.g., learning English versus needing support in phonemic awareness or number sense).

When your teams use the matrix, they specify

- the tools or data they plan to use for screening.

- who will administer the assessments.

- when the assessments will be done (e.g., windows of time for assessment).

Making explicit these decisions in advance helps ensure that proper professional development can be provided for assessors and that time blocks and other logistics for assessing are built into the master calendar. Your team will also take care to record instances when screening data are collected outside the regularly scheduled windows. For example, your team may specify that screening data are to be collected for new students within their first week of entering the school, including those students who enter at unexpected times, such as after a foster care placement in your school neighborhood or a student who moves in and out of a juvenile detention facility. Remember, creating a culture of welcome and belonging for all students means providing access to all students—and that belief pushes us to plan ahead as well as be flexible in the moment.

Based on the tools your team lists on their matrix, they next specify the decision rules that ease and provide consistency in deciding when students need additional and intensified support resources to meet their needs. Earlier we talked about avoiding decision fatigue on the part of educators and their teams. Establishing clear decision rules helps most educators avoid fatigue (particularly during challenging times—the week before spring break, for example ☺). Most screening assessments come with their own research-based decision rules that help teams interpret data and accurately predict the likelihood a student needs more support than most other students. In the absence of recommended decision rules, teams make their decision-making process transparent and closely monitor the effects of their self-defined rules. (For those of you who need to know more about screening, we recommend the chapter by our colleagues Lane, Oakes, and Menzies in Pullen & Kennedy, 2019.)

Key to effective use of the tiered instruction matrix is the ability to move away from too many data sources. You may know from experience this is very difficult for some educators to do, especially if they have been using a source for many years. Check out the field trip here about how one school grappled with what to include in their matrix.

FIELD TRiP

"WHAT I NEED" IN TIERED INSTRUCTION MATRIX

One school had a matrix they populated with the district-supported screening tools and decision rules. Their screening tools had a sufficient level of technical adequacy for screening decisions and well-established decision rules for students needing additional support in either literacy or mathematics or both. They didn't, however, have decision rules that applied to students who exceeded benchmarks. The team had to grapple with this gap in their system. They decided to create a block of time in the schedule that could be personalized for each student. The data reviews they conducted to determine who needed additional support would start with students approaching a benchmark and then move to identifying a next best step for all other students. The established block of time in the schedule was called "WIN–What I Need" time. (Isn't that an awesome name for an added block of time to be used flexibly during the day?). This time was used to identify what learning need was there and appropriately teach to that need. As they started implementing WIN time, they started to see a pattern in how data were used, and they were then able to fill in their matrix. Over time, they came up with a threshold in literacy and math that seemed like a reasonable indicator to use for targeting skill areas in meaningful ways (e.g., students who earned below a 70% on the unit test or who repeatedly indicated confusion through their exit ticket card). You can watch one of our teacher heroes demonstrate this great method at https://www.teachingchannel.org/video/daily-lesson-assessment. They noted those decision rules in a different color from the district-provided ones, so that they would be sure to monitor for any unintended consequences from their choices. They also alerted the district to be on the lookout for new screening tools that might help them more efficiently address students who were exceeding benchmarks.

For middle and high schools, often screening tool authors recommend using a gated process rather than universal screening (e.g., Van Norman, Nelson, & Klingbeil, 2017). With a gated process, teams simultaneously review attendance, course grades, grade point average (GPA), and historical data in academics, behavior, and social-emotional learning. When they see an indication of risk, the team usually collects additional information to determine whether support may be warranted, and if so, of what kind. An indication of risk might be not passing one or more unit tests at the nine-week mark. In order for the team to make a good match with resources, they may collect additional data to ensure the struggle isn't due to a lack of foundational reading skills.

For example, in one large high school, a school team created their own early warning system that allowed them to look at the data sources we referenced above. They were able to set thresholds that would send the team a list of students who met one or more criteria they specified. For example, if a student was near to missing 10% of instructional days, then the system would notify the team. Likewise, teams would receive notification after the first progress report if a student was failing or close to failing one or more classes. This nimble system allowed them to be detectives with the data and determine whether additional data might help them make decisions about student support. Once we have an indication that we need to be responsive, we can go deeper to understand and match support resources.

Here in Figure 2.5 is an example from Wolf Creek Elementary School.

School/District: **Wolf Creek Elementary** Grade(s): **K - 5**   Date:

Curricular Area: ☒Literacy ☐Mathmatics ☐Behavior/Social Emotional Learning

Part 1: Universal Support	
What	District standards document click here. Curriculum map by quarter click here. Instructional and differentiation framework click here. Recommended lesson plan template click here.
When	Each grade level ELA block and supporting personnel depicted on master schedule

Part 2: Universal Screening			
Tools	**Who Administers**	**When Administered**	
DIBELS MAP	Classroom Teacher with staff covering classroom during assessments	Fall/Winter/Spring	
	Additional Support		**Intensified Support**	

	...to meet benchmark	...when exceeding benchmark	...to meet benchmark	...when exceeding benchmark
Decision Rules	If DIBELS Composite and/or subtest indicator yellow and/or MAP below 40th %ile... then consider best match from instructions listed below	If DIBELS Composite indicator green AND MAP above 75th %ile... then consider best match from instructions listed below	If DIBELS Composite and/or subtest indicator red and/or MAP below 20th %ile... then consider best match from instructions listed below AND Intensified Support options	If DIBELS Composite indicator green and MAP above 90th %ile... then consider best match from instructions listed below AND Intensified Support options

Source: SWIFT Education Center (2016).

Figure 2.5. Universal support and screening example

TAKiNG IT TO THE TEAM

UNIVERSAL SUPPORT AND SCREENING

- What are the important conversations to have about the shared understanding of our universal support first instruction, universal screening, and decision rules?

- What are the current strengths of our universal support, screening, and decision rules related to all learners?

- Did we miss any student groups when we developed our universal support or screening tools? Who are they, and how can they be included?

- Have we made decisions about what to do if a screening tool is not matched to our student population?

- Look at that student list you made in the Introduction. Are any additional conversations needed related to our universal support and screening systems when we think about students on our lists?

MY THOUGHTS

MATRIX PART 3: INSTRUCTION AND SUPPORT

An important aspect of building equitable MTSS is making sure students are matched to need-based instruction and support in a timely manner. The matrix helps guide the team toward this goal by prompting them to specifying broad skill areas that may require more instruction or support than the universal tier provides. In the area of literacy, these might be skills like phonological awareness, phonics, fluency, comprehension, and vocabulary. Teams recommend resources and arrangements to specifically target each skill area. Doesn't sound like a big deal, does it? It kind of is. OK, it really is.

This part of the matrix helps articulate what resources are best used to address different needs. What starts to happen is that teams have conversations about the *function* a resource serves, not *whom* it serves. This shift is true even in middle and high schools, where discussions about phonological awareness, phonics, fluency, comprehension, and vocabulary are less prevalent. When resources are established to target skills and are made available within each grade level, we begin to see a comprehensive system of support come into focus.

Think back to the process of resource mapping. We didn't ask you to think about your coworkers by their organizational silos or role categories. Likewise, on this part of the matrix, we ask you not to describe things like "Title I instructional supports," or "special education instructional supports." Rather, document a specific list of resources and choices to address different academic, behavioral, and social-emotional needs. Categorize these choices by the skill areas they address, not by a student label or entitlement status for additional services.

We want to make this point with added emphasis: *Teams select instruction and support to meet identified skill needs, not based on other student characteristics.*

This idea is equity at its most basic and profound. Think of this in the same way you might think when you go to doctor. You want your doctor to assess your symptoms, gather data, and make a decision about what treatment you need based upon those variables, rather than your finances (funding source), or previous diagnosis (label), or even perceptions about your race, history, et cetera. Likewise, teams need to specify what skill needs are met with the different instructional materials, methods, and supports. As shown in the example below, a team identified four possible resources to use when a student demonstrates need to improve reading fluency. The matrix facilitates quick decision making by providing a curated set of options specific to the need, rather than a long laundry list of all reading support options. Our experience is that the extra step clarifying the skill area addressed by each option helps prevent inappropriate matching.

For example, without the specificity of skill area, teams eager to provide early intervention may select a fluency intervention for a student who has a need in the area of phonics. Such a mismatch is dangerous for a number of reasons, not the least of which is a student spending several weeks continuing to practice misrules with phonics, which makes the eventual task of unlearning even more difficult for the student and the teacher. While we make the best decision we can based on the information we have at the time, the specification of skill area and instructional match is an added layer of prevention and efficiency for MTSS.

Take a look at the literacy example in Figure 2.6. If you are a middle or high school educator, think about how instruction around missing literacy skills may come into play within subject-specific course content. As students get a little older, we may begin to think that skills that should have been developed at a younger age are not our responsibility. Challenge yourself here with this thought: Equity-based MTSS involves accountability at all grade levels to address the full array of student need. If we plan with the expectation that some students may need some critical literacy skills, even at middle or high school, we are not left struggling to meet a need in the moment. For example, it is helpful (actually important) for high school teachers to know the routine that was taught in elementary school around approaching multisyllabic words. Why? That routine is a great way to easily ensure accessibility of a new science vocabulary with words like amphiprotic, anhydride, coagulation, and delocalization. Be prepared to scaffold reading these words with such prompts as these: (1) Look for word parts at the beginning, (2) the end, (3) and then the vowels; (4) say the parts, (5) say the word fast, and (6) make it a real word (Archer, Gleason, & Vachon, 2000). Doing something like this allows the students to start owning the word, so they can then focus on where you are going next with them in understanding the meaning and application of the word. This also reminds students that there was an important purpose of all that practice with the routine in elementary school, and that purpose is becoming evident now that they are learning words that may be linked to big and important future careers! The matrix allows for development in common broad skill areas as well as less common areas (full array of student need) across all grade levels.

Part 3: Instruction and Support

Area identified for support	Who Provides		When Provided
	Available personnel as identified on Master Schedule		Available time as identified on Master Schedule
	Additional Support		**Intensified Support**
	...to meet benchmark	...when exceeding benchmark	options to consider
Phonics	Wonders Tier II lesson First Grade PALS EIR Skill specific lesson Sound Partners Corrective Reading	Skill specific lessons Targeted Centers	Considerations for Universal and Additional Tiers Increase frequency or duration of additional support Change arrangements
Phonemic Awareness	Wonders Tier II lesson KPALS Ladders to Literacy	Skill specific lessons Targeted Centers	Increase and vary positive corrective feedback Increase and vary opportunities to respond
Fluency	Wonders Tier II lesson Read Naturally Repeated Readings Six-Minute Solutions Quick Reads Readers Theater	Readers' Theater Targeted Centers	Break tasks into segments with specific focus goals Provide scaffolds Include strategies for self-monitoring
Vocabulary	Wonders Tier II lesson Mini lesson Multiple Meaning Words	Skill-specific lessons Targeted Centers	Attend to opportunities to generalize and integrate
Comprehension	PALS FAST ForWord Cognitive processing strategies	Literature circles Skill-specific lessons Targeted Centers	

Source: SWIFT Education Center (2016).

Figure 2.6. **Additional instruction and support example**

Expect wide variation in the resources listed in the additional support column. The options you list in this part of the matrix may include a combination of commercially available solutions (e.g., Math 180), support routines (e.g., repeated readings), or instructional protocols (e.g., I Do, We Do, You Do) that guide selection (or design) of the best support for the student need. Some teams choose to list support options in a hierarchy of least intense to most intense. For example, using a repeated reading protocol for fluency is less intense than participating in Read Naturally. Others create a subsidiary document that provides more specifics to aid the selection process (e.g., format of support, recommended lesson length, or subject recommendation).

The intensified tier of an equity-based MTSS differs from many traditional tiered support schema. Like others, we hold to the importance of the intensified tier being provided along with access to universal and additional support. However, we encourage teams to take an instructional approach to intensification. It is our experience that often additional and intensified support is made available based on characteristics of the named tier (i.e., Tier 2 always equals more time, or Tier 3 always uses a special educator or reading specialist). Our approach, in contrast, asks teams to specify the universal support components and all supplemental supports, regardless of time or comprehensive nature, in the additional tier.

In the additional tier, you aren't just adding something; instead view this as a continuum that is based on what you are learning about the students. It's more than making time and personnel available; it's about more than picking from a list of instructional materials that you selected. This tier is about further individualizing your approach. Treat variables like time, personnel, and instructional strategies as components to be considered for an individual student. Look to see what the data indicate; don't just pick another support, add more time, or reteach the same skill in a different place. Carefully plan appropriate support based on what you learn from the data.

Then, the highest tier of support gives you a way to think about "intensifying" both universal and additional support, that is, specifying how you are intensifying universal instruction and/or an added support (Figure 2.7). This approach represents a very strong and important tie to equity. *Intensify* is a verb. We are asking you to intensify universal and/or additional support to meet identified and understood needs. *Intensify* is not a noun—not a different place, person, or thing. When we engage our teams in a process of intensifying, we remain focused on those things we have control over and that move the needle on student outcomes. Teams may recommend options related to grouping arrangements, instructional methods, feedback, frequency or duration of instruction, and so on.

FIELD TRiP

A middle school team with grade-level and special educators started thinking about how to improve their data protocol around additional and intensified support. They built time into their master schedule for a team review of progress of all student groups who received additional support and to determine whether and what changes were warranted. In the beginning, their discussions mainly focused on the questions, " Did we make the right match for each student?" and "Are we consistently providing the planned support?" Over time, they were confident and on target with these questions.

(Continued)

(Continued)

Their next questions then revolved around, "What do we do when progress is adequate?" and "What do we do when progress is indicating we need to change something?" The answer to the former question was often a positive for the team, while the answer to the latter was more humbling and moved them into discussion about how to tweak the support (more time, more opportunities to respond) or select a different support resource from the list. While the team was made up of amazing, well-intentioned educators, their response was more often about their own *accountability* than it was a *deep down response* that would move the needle and bring about results that would be meaningful now and in the future for the student.

Their discussions helped them realize they needed to shift and dig deeper. They needed to make their data routine more about, "What do we know now about this student that will help us think about intensifying our efforts to support learning?" When they asked this question, the teachers looked at what they formatively understood about student strengths and needs in the context of their daily lesson plans in "chunks" (e.g., Wonders Day One: Introduce the concept, listening comprehension, vocabulary; or REWARDS: Blending parts into words, vowel combinations, vowel conversions, reading parts of real words, correcting close approximations using contexts). As the team members practiced and evolved this process over time, they often vocalized how they were starting to feel as if they were really doing effective student planning that embedded the individualization in a way that wasn't simply layering on "more."

We'd be remiss if we didn't share that the team always ended the data meetings by asking, "How did we support each other as we all attempt to ensure we are supporting students?" A cool team ritual—wouldn't you say?

	Part 3: Instruction and Support		
	Who Provides		**When Provided**
	Available personnel as identified on master schedule		Available time as identified on master schedule
Area identified for support	**Additional Support**		**Intensified Support**
	...to meet benchmark	...when exceeding benchmark	options to consider
Phonics	Wonders Tier II lesson First Grade PALS EIR Skill specific lesson Sound Partners Corrective Reading	Skill specific lessons Targeted Centers	Considerations for Universal and Additional Tiers Increase frequency or duration of additional support Change arrangements
Phonemic Awareness	Wonders Tier II lesson KPALS Ladders to Literacy	Skill specific lessons Targeted Centers	Increase and vary positive corrective feedback Increase and vary opportunities to respond
Fluency	Wonders Tier II lesson Read Naturally Repeated Readings Six-Minute Solutions Quick Reads Readers Theater	Readers' Theater Targeted Centers	Break tasks into segments with specific focus goals Provide scaffolds Include strategies for self-monitoring
Vocabulary	Wonders Tier II lesson Mini lesson Multiple Meaning Words	Skill-specific lessons Targeted Centers	Attend to opportunities to generalize and integrate
Comprehension	PALS FAST ForWord Cognitive processing strategies	Literature circles Skill-specific lessons Targeted Centers	

Source: SWIFT Education Center (2016).

Figure 2.7. **Intensified instruction and support example**

TAKiNG IT TO THE TEAM

ADDITIONAL AND INTENSIFIED SUPPORT

- Given the way the matrix articulates additional and intensified support, how might it positively influence an equitable approach to addressing needs of learners?

- What are strengths of our instruction and support section of the matrix? What is missing?

(Continued)

(Continued)

- Do we have all we need in terms of professional learning and resources for educators to know how to take an instructional approach to intensified support?

- Grab the student list you made in the Introduction. Are any additional conversations needed related to what we have identified for additional or intensified support for the students on our lists?

- (For middle and high school educators) In what ways might we embed core literacy or mathematics skills that may not have been achieved early within our content-specific courses?

MY THOUGHTS

MATRIX PART 4: PROGRESS MONITORING

The last section of the matrix provides a place for your team to specify the tools, logistics, and decision rules associated with progress monitoring (Figure 2.8). A defining component of MTSS is the practice of engaging in formative evaluation of progress so you can make decisions to adjust support in a timely fashion. You never fully know beforehand what instruction and support will work for an individual student. As it did when listing universal screening tools, logistics, and decision rules, your team articulates a process that allows all adults in the school to have a common understanding of how you plan to respond to patterns in student performance data.

Part 4: Progress Monitoring		
Tools	**Who Administers**	**When Administered**
Acadience Reading subtest matched to instruction Assessments embedded in instruction General Outcome Measures, as appropriate Other measures when necessary	Instructional Specialist	Acadience Reading subtest matched to instruction—embedded in instruction 2-4x month Embedded instruction : Weekly or Additional Supports Daily for Intensified Supports General Outcome Measures 1x per month Other measures frequency identified by teacher/team

	Additional Support		Intensified Support	
	...to meet benchmark	...when exceeding benchmark	...to meet benchmark	...when exceeding benchmark
Decision Rules	If progress monitoring tool indicates 3 consecutive data points at or above proficiency, then consider exiting the instruction If 3 consecutive data points indicate lack of sufficient progress, then consider adjusting instruction or begin Intensified Support	Individually determine decision rules that fit best for the additional support provided.	If 3 consecutive data points indicate lack of sufficient progress, then consider adjusting Intensified Support If 3 consecutive data points demonstrate sufficient progress, consider whether to continue or reduce supports.	Individually determine decision rules that fit best for the intensified support provided.

Source: SWIFT Education Center (2016).

Figure 2.8. **Progress monitoring example**

We emphasize the importance of selecting progress monitoring tools that have established reliability and validity for the purpose of evaluating adequacy of progress. Just as you want your universal screening indicators to provide a trustworthy indication of the likelihood a student will need additional support, you will want your progress monitoring tools to provide trustworthy information about when to maintain a course of action, when that action may no longer be necessary, and when to consider making a change to support you are providing. We want to be very clear about this: Use the data to indicate when *you* need to make a change. In early years of tiered support systems, a heavy emphasis was on the use of data to describe the student's response to intervention. While the data represent how a student is responding, we are steadfast in our focus on finding the instructional match that enables learning to high levels. The system indicates when *we adults need do something in response to the data.*

We recommend thinking about progress monitoring backward and forward: progress monitoring and monitoring of progress. Let us explain.

Progress monitoring is a way to assess student growth that has been demonstrated to be technically sound for this purpose. Examples include measures included in different data systems such as Fastbridge, Acadience, and Aimsweb, or in different types of curriculum-based measures. Monitoring of progress, on the other hand, can be considered types of assessment that may be helpful in the instructional decision-making process but are not necessarily scientifically validated. These may include teacher observations, exit tickets, intervention-embedded assessments, work samples, and so on.

Similar to the decision rules for universal screening, progress monitoring decision rules denote when to continue what you are doing and when to change. When the research is not clear, teams should make their best recommendation based on the information known at the time. It is important to be able to be transparent about the nature of the evidence you have and the tools you use when sharing the results with families. Remember, we are all working together to make the best scenario we can for student learning.

One of the most powerful bodies of research related to the effects of progress monitoring came out of the work of Stan Deno and colleagues at the University of Minnesota known as curriculum-based measures (CBM). While now known by different names and not always linked directly to a curriculum, the concept of validating reliable measures that could serve as indicators of growth across short increments of time with the purpose of informing instructional practices remains a hallmark of Deno and those who studied under him during the past 30-plus years (Espin, McMaster, Rose, & Wayman, 2012).

Upon completion of the matrix, your team might summarize areas that a leadership team could add to a list for exploration that would strengthen MTSS decision making. For example, a team may recognize a need for a stronger screening tool or process to identify students who may need additional support in areas related to social-emotional learning. Or your team may want to expand the available options that address conceptual issues related to mathematics. The team can outline in the matrix the best approach at a point in time, but they can also make plans to revisit any part of it when policies, research, and accumulated knowledge provide an opportunity to improve.

TAKING IT TO THE TEAM

PROGRESS MONITORING

- What are the important conversations to have about the shared understanding of progress monitoring tools and decision rules?

- What are current strengths of our progress monitoring tools and decision rules related to all learners?

- For students with extensive need for support, are we intensifying the two-way communication support with their families?

- Remember your list of students? Are any additional conversations needed related to what we have identified for progress monitoring for students on our lists?

MY THOUGHTS

We invite you to take a pause and hear Angie's "Why MTSS." She has perspectives as a sister and educator. Megan might be a bit surprised to see what an impact she had on her big sister's entire professional career! We are inspired; we hope you are too.

FIELD TRiP

ANGIE'S WHY MTSS

My why for this work began when my youngest sister entered school. Megan is six and a half years younger than I. Learning was always difficult for her, as was expressing her thoughts and emotions. Megan's kindergar ten teacher commented that she just couldn't get Megan to talk—but at home, believe me, she talked nonstop. That was the year when the school determined that she needed special education services, and my memories of her include lots of tears, frustration, and confusion. The nightly homework was painstaking. Our other sister and I would help when we could, but sometimes we just couldn't explain the concepts or steps in a way that made sense to Megan. Her social skills were really no better, and her social development wasn't made easier by the fact that Megan attended a special program that was moved a few times, so Megan had to change schools over and over again. For someone who had difficulty socially expressing herself, this constant change was devastating. How could she make and maintain any friendships if the environment kept changing?

My why for pursuing equity in education? It began with Megan. What if education support had been provided differently? What if she had been able to participate with her peers, in her home school, for her entire school life? As a senior in college, I realized that I wanted to help students like my sister—that's when my dreams of changing education began.

3

• • •

ENGINEERING YOUR MTSS

> The master schedule is to a school what grading policies are to teachers and classrooms. It reveals the true beliefs, attitudes, values, and priorities of the school. The school's master schedule is like looking at an MRI of the inner workings of a school. It is the window to the soul of the school.
>
> —NATIONAL ASSOCIATION OF SECONDARY SCHOOL PRINCIPALS (2011, P. 1)

We have a foundation (Chapter 1) and a structural frame (Chapter 2). Now it is time to engineer the way the water and electricity flow around the house—you know, plumbing and wiring (Figure 3.1). But in the case of your new construction, we are going to think about the way resources and people flow around the school through the use of a master schedule.

ENGiNEERING

Figure 3.1. Engineering MTSS

REVISIT WHAT AND WHY

In Chapter 1, a thorough resource mapping process launched the work of equity-based MTSS. In Chapter 2, some of those resources were used in constructing a tiered instruction matrix to aid decision making about instruction and support. We'll now revisit some of the other things you inventoried, like the time allocations and requirements, in order to connect to the master schedule work we will discuss here.

However, before creating their MTSS-driven master schedule, we encourage teams to reflect on what beliefs, attitudes, values, and priorities are reflected in their *current* master schedule. Not only examine a completed master schedule, but also reflect on the process of how that schedule was created. In some schools, the master schedule is left up to each grade-level team; in others it is created by the related arts teachers (e.g., music, art, PE, library, computers); and in others the principal or school counselor conducts the process. As the quotation at the opening of this chapter suggests, the schedule and the process by which it is created provide a window into your school values.

How do the values of equity-based MTSS lead to a master schedule that is different from others? Our experience is that schedules are often developed annually to articulate order and structure for a school, rather than approached as a strategy for accomplishing important educational outcomes. When the master schedule is approached as a variable that can be changed, teams realize the power they have to adjust time, people, and spaces in a way that is dynamic and flexible. (Do you hear those words from our definition of equity?) Does this approach mean the schedule is constantly changing? Likely not. Just as we mentioned earlier, when thinking about moving people and resources, educators can get nervous about what this change could mean. Fear of the unknown begins to emerge. Once you get several heads wrapped around the five steps below, you have a safety net for thinking, creating, and adjusting your schoolwide schedule. Then your master schedule can be used to create equitable access for all students to receive what they need, and create conditions under which teachers can plan and deliver to meet complex and changing student needs.

Developing a schedule that is student-centered means that careful strategizing has to take place as it is created. Here's how we suggest you do it.

HOW TO DO A MTSS MASTER SCHEDULE

The strategy for developing a master schedule involves five steps (Figure 3.2):

1. Understand what you want for your students

2. Understand your student needs

3. Understand your current reality

4. Revisit your strengths

5. Match strengths to needs

Your team can think about the strategy and process of planning an equity-based MTSS master schedule by imagining they are meeting in a "situation room"—you know, a room where real-time intelligence and support are provided to the president and key staff to make crucial decisions. This is the room where they deepen their understanding of important things, where they think and plan with intention and aim to make the best decisions they can with the information they have at the time. This is a room where things get done!

While we imagine the nation's situation room is high tech (or looks that way on television), you can get the job done with sticky wall chart paper, a big white board, or a shared Google Document, or if you want high tech, you can do that too. This simple format allows a team to keep key pieces of information in mind as the schedule is designed.

The first step in the strategy is understanding what you want for all your students. What are your beliefs, values, priorities, and desires? When others look at the schedule you create, they will see these values reflected in how you spend your time and allocate resources. In Chapter 1, we introduced the foundational transformation in action practices for implementing and sustaining equity-based MTSS. When teams articulate what they want, they engage in a design activity that may be revisited during the master schedule process, with particular attention paid to those things that influence their scheduling decisions. You may already have a school vision statement that can serve in the same way. For example, your team may check to see, "Do we value and specify the importance of collaborative planning time for our teachers?" "Do we ideally want to ensure all students have access to all courses and activities, regardless of their need for extra support?" "Is our whole staff committed to being flexible with their time and talents in order to meet student needs?" These questions and answers can be listed on the first of your five wall charts.

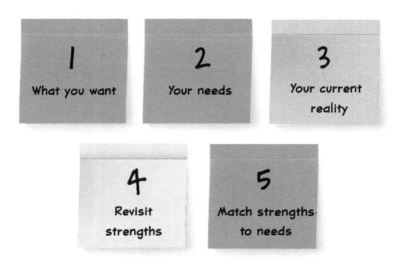

Figure 3.2. Master schedule development

The second step in the strategy is understanding your needs. How? Your schoolwide data are essential to your understanding. Although your team is probably accustomed to analyzing student data with an eye toward instructional needs, we recommend your team relook at the data and capture observations related to the school schedule. Your team can use spring semester data to develop a decent schedule to begin fall semester. After fall screening data are collected, it is hoped that only minor schedule adjustments will be needed.

During this data review, a team might realize that a group of students does not have access to courses they need to graduate on time, and so the team may decide to change the master schedule to remedy the situation before it turns into students enrolling in summer school or credit recovery programs. Further, teams might realize some students don't have equitable access to supporting arts classes, like music, and work to remedy this inequity. As another example, the math department team may recognize that the number of students who demonstrate need for additional support exceeds what is possible to accommodate with current staff and small-group instruction. They may decide to alter the master schedule to allow for new approaches to teaching and learning, such as pairing grade-level teachers with special educators, during a content instruction period. Think about how schoolwide student data might reveal intense needs that can be better met by thoughtful construction of the school's master schedule. What can you do differently with scheduling and staffing? A bulleted list of your observations and ideas goes on the second of your five wall charts.

The third step in creating an equitable MTSS schedule is to capture your current reality. This step has two parts and is a bit of a shuffle. The first thing to do is list state or district requirements related to time—or refresh what you prepared for your resource map. (It is to be hoped that the purpose of resource mapping is becoming clear!) Mark the things that you know are "a must" related to allocation of time, such as negotiated contractual plan time, required recess time per state guidelines, and so on. Next, make a second list of your current space assignments and personnel that have scheduling limitations—pulling from and updating your resource map again. For example, you may have a speech pathologist available in your school on Monday, Wednesday, and Friday. Or you may have to schedule physical education classes before 10:55 and after 12:45 because the gymnasium also serves as the cafeteria. You get the idea—there are parts of the schedule that are outside your control to change. Really challenge yourself though. Maybe that speech pathologist could change her days. "It has always been this way" is not outside of your control to suggest a change.

The fourth step in the master schedule process involves teams revisiting the other components of their resource map and making current notes on their thoughts about other strengths that have scheduling implications. For example, they might think about staff who are available at various times during the day. When the schoolwide student support needs start to take shape, this review will help the team be in a stronger position to make staffing matches for universal, additional, and intensified support roles. Another example is consideration about which spaces might lend themselves to alternative teaching arrangements. Because the equity-based MTSS approach to scheduling embraces a view that the whole system needs to be dynamic and alive, everyone in the system quickly learns to anticipate changes to physical, instructional, scheduling, and staffing arrangements as student needs change over time.

Our experience tells us that your team might appreciate developing a master schedule that is set up in five-minute increments (yikes! we know). This level of detail allows teams to think about how to utilize personnel for portions of time, rather than in course blocks. For example, a coteaching arrangement in fourth grade may require scheduling various roles for each individual during a small-group portion of a reading block, let's say from 10:00 to 10:30—right in the middle of the 9:20–10:50 literacy block. The implication is that one of these coteachers is available to do something else from 9:20 to 10:00. Basically, this step should culminate in a list of the personnel who are potentially available across the school day, the spaces that could be leveraged for different arrangements, and other strengths that should be considered before drafting a master schedule.

Finally, your team takes the notes captured in the previous four steps and starts determining how to use a strengths- and student-centered approach to building a schedule. This five-step exercise helps schools to be flexible in how they use personnel, space, and time to meet identified student needs and create a school climate that supports teachers as well as students. If you don't have a tool to develop your schedule in five-minute increments, we have a simple spreadsheet you can download and make your own (see https://tinyurl.com/SWIFTschedulingtool).

Our experience tells us that some of you right now would like to close the book because this task is quite arduous. For some, the level of detail required here is simply painful and seemingly never ending. The good news is that there are always individuals on the school team who actually enjoy this maze of information. (Really, perhaps you are one of them. ☺) They approach it like a complex puzzle that needs solving. This is the time to engage those who enjoy piecing the solution together while holding close the values and beliefs of those who may not be directly constructing the schedule itself. A master schedule that builds upon all the strengths and talents in the school, while honoring the culture and climate of the school, helps to enable an equitable MTSS.

TAKING IT TO THE TEAM

MTSS MASTER SCHEDULE

- Do we feel our values and beliefs are reflected in our current master schedule? Why or why not?

- What are things we would change about our master schedule that would meet needs differently?

- How do we feel when we think about changing the schedule?

- How might the process outlined in this chapter allow our team to think differently about people, places, and how students are served?

- Who do we see as key team members for developing the strategy behind scheduling? Do we know the people in our system who enjoy this task?

MY THOUGHTS

As we think about reworking the master schedule, we have another big equity opportunity. Have we looked at our values, our why, our design, and made sure to carry through those belief structures into scheduling? This is where the challenge to do what we believe starts to take shape, because the master schedule (the soul of the school) will be the direct reflection of just that.

Meet Cokethea, yet another inspiring educator and mom. Take a look at her why.

FIELD TRiP

COKETHEA'S WHY MTSS

Far too many students of color are failing in America's educational system. Disparities in their educational experiences and outcomes are evident as early as kindergarten and persist along every major step in the journey toward high school graduation. As an educator of color with a rising kindergartener, I look at his excitement, curiosity, and wonderment, and I know that my hopes and dreams for my child are like any other parent's. We want a school system that will give our children the greatest odds of being successful! From my personal experience working in schools, I know so many amazing, dedicated, and passionate teachers and school leaders who work tirelessly to close gaps, to increase achievement, and to build authentic, meaningful relationships with families.

What often is missing for teachers, administrators, and families is a comprehensive framework to ensure equity, so each student receives the necessary support to experience success in the classroom. An equity-based multi-tiered system of support is just such a framework—and it recognizes the power of student agency and family voice while building the capacity of teachers and school leaders to work collaboratively to elevate teaching, learning, and student outcomes. I believe in this model for schools, because it recognizes that all students should have their needs uniquely matched to the supports that will help them thrive and succeed. This is what I want for my kid, because he is unique, special, and deserving of a world-class educational system to meet his emerging needs!

4

• • •

MAKING IT YOUR OWN MTSS

Data have no meaning. Meaning is imposed through interpretation.

—WELLMAN AND LIPTON (2000, P. 47)

It is time to move in! We laid a strong foundation, set up structural elements, and put in the plumbing and electrical wiring. Now comes the fun part. You get to make it your own (Figure 4.1). You get to individualize it, make it unique to your context and culture. We know there are other things to do, like painting the walls, hanging pictures, selecting furniture, and so on. But you have a sound structure built by your team, for your team, and together you will make it increasingly beautiful and comfortable over time.

You can turn on the lights, open the door, and start living in the new space you created. The kids are here, and you can begin to measure their needs and match resources to them. This is where educators really get to shine! They make this place we call school their own, put their spin on it, color it up, and move things around to meet the needs of the day or the year. Most important, because of all this previous work, you have time to make it your own, to modify and adjust.

The last thing we have to share with your team will help you keep track of all the details that you put on the "honey-do list," as this metaphorical house becomes your home. Literally, we mean the things you will do as your school becomes fluid, responsive, and dynamic and uses all available resources matched to each student's need.

MAKE iT YOUR OWN

Source: SWIFT Education Center (2016).

Figure 4.1. **Make it your own MTSS**

The last tool we want you and your team to learn to use is a data routine for **resource matching**. But first, we need to make a really important visit back to why we want to keep our eyes on equity. With the definition of equity we provided in the Introduction, we can't simply end with a tool that maps resources with data without ensuring we have returned to our core values. We started by paying attention to our words, our actions, and our environment, and by ensuring that each and every student *recognizes* that they are welcome, they belong, and they matter. Period.

We use the word *recognize* intentionally—students need to overtly see, hear, and recognize they belong and they matter. These sentiments can't just be what is in our hearts or in our minds. They need to outwardly show. Those of us who are parents know that our kids pay attention to what we do, not just what we say. The same applies at school. When students have a grade-level peer with a significant disability in their classroom, they need to see that our system and all the adults in it recognize this peer belongs there. When a child's native language is honored, it affects the degree to which the child is perceived as being welcomed. When staff take inventory to ensure that every student has an adult in the building who knows something important about them beyond their test scores and course grades, it shows each student matters.

When equity is our compass's true north, and our hearts and minds are set on making sure our system works for all students, then we can enter into a resource matching process that allows us to understand and bring the best curricular, instructional, and other needed support to a dynamic and fluid learning environment where growth happens!

TAKiNG IT TO THE TEAM

WELCOME AND BELONGING MATTER

- In what ways do we show students they are welcomed, they belong, and they matter at our school?

- Remember the list you made in the Introduction? How do those students know they are welcomed, belong, and matter? Do they have this experience with many adults and peers in our school. or is it just one?

- Reflect again for a moment on spaces. Are there some students who are segregated based on label, race, funding source, discipline, or something else?

- Have we promoted equity in our access, engagement, and opportunity for each and every student?

MY THOUGHTS

Before we dig into resource matching using a data routine, we want to give you the opportunity to go on another field trip. On this trip, you meet C. J. and see one way a high school worked to create a sense of belonging. This practice allowed educators to really know students as they entered into conversations around data.

FIELD TRiP

EACH AND EVERY STUDENT

It was at an MTSS professional development session that we met a principal of a high school in a rural midwestern community. He was sharing that part of the culture building at his high school involves establishing and sharing in a Google folder a set of "student profile pages" for each student in the school (Figure 4.2). Staff are able to access each page and enter positive things they learn about students—their gifts, interests, aspirations, and so on. As a leader in the school, the principal is able to monitor these pages and make sure each and every student has an adult in the school who knows something meaningful about them. If he finds a student who does not have such a relationship, he takes on that responsibility. He shared, "We are constantly working diligently to improve our relationships both within and outside the walls of our buildings." When it comes to MTSS, he explained, "While MTSS is a process that could take years to develop, we feel that by being proactive in our efforts to build positive relationships, we can deter from 'below the line' behavior and teach 'above the line' behavior."

C.J. Hughes
- Made All-State Band last year—plays trombone
- Loves basketball
- He has a dog named "Diamond" who is very good at catching a frisbee
- Loves to fish with his Grandpa
- Works hard and earns good grades

Figure 4.2. **Student profile**

RESOURCE MATCHING

Okay, so we constantly work to create a welcoming environment and maintain a solid sense of belonging. We planned ahead on our tiered instruction matrix for how resources can be used to meet diverse student needs, and we have some student data that helped us frame a master schedule. How, then, do we move to actually matching the various resources to actual student needs? This is where we move to the resource matching tool (Figure 4.3) and data routines to ensure timely matches get made and enacted.

Schools use resource matching as a way to communicate and coordinate instructional support based on data from their particular students. These plans are continuously reviewed and adjusted in light of screening and progress monitoring data, and may lead to adjustments in the master schedule and resource allocations as student needs change.

So the next thing we show you is how to use data routines to feed your resource matching tool.

RESOURCE MATCHiNG

School/District:		Grade(s): 1		Date:

Curricular Area: ☒ Literacy ☐ Mathmatics ☐ Behavior/Social Emotional Learning

Area of Need	Student Group	Instructor	Time	Location
Phonics	Wonders Tier II mini lessons Joe, Tiffany, Chris, Clifton, Mark Fast ForWord Mark	CJ AP	8:30 - 9:00 8:30 - 9:00	1st Grade Classroom Computer Lab
Phonemic Awareness	KPALS Jack, Leah, Greg	MK	8:30 - 9:15	Library
Vocabulary	Early Vocabulary Connections Maria	JD	8:30 - 9:00	Library

Source: **SWIFT Education Center (2016).**

Figure 4.3. **Resource matching example**

DATA ROUTINES

Are you ready for your system to work with efficiency and ease, knowing that the MTSS load-bearing walls support your actions in every part of your school, grade level, or department? Student data provide you a snapshot of your current reality, allow you to respond in a timely manner, and provide an indicator for progress monitoring that promotes continuous improvement.

We approach data with these basic understandings:

- Data are used to answer questions and create more questions. (Why can't it be simple? ☺)

- Error is always present in data. (Just expect it; it'll be okay. ☺)

- People, not data, make decisions—thank goodness. (See bullet above. ☺)

- Know your truth—you have to decide what data you want to use (because there is so much ☺).

- Equity-check it. (Keep an eye for equity on data at all times.)

Why approach it with these maxims? Because they help us to handle the myriad of data sources that come our way. Because they keep us grounded in the important role we have as educators when we engage in data-informed decision making. They remind us of our role in understanding what questions we are trying to answer. They maintain a focus on understanding data in the context of our reality. They remind us that measurement is complex and that we own the analysis and resulting decisions. That's why. (Were we too serious? We didn't mean to scare you.) When you put data reviews into action, we think you will find they can be invigorating, empowering, and even exciting, because, once again, this is a system (data) that is built into our structure (MTSS) to create efficiency and effectiveness in support.

For MTSS, we suggest this data routine—our data mantra, if you will: Organize, Process, Act (Figure 4.4). (OK—this wasn't intentional, but it does have a nice Greek celebratory ring to it! OPA!)

DATA ROUTiNES

Source: SWIFT Education Center (2016).

Figure 4.4. Data routine

Here's the really awesome part. This data routine is to be used across the entire system, whether a school team is approaching and developing a plan for schoolwide use, or a department or grade-level group is strengthening its universal tier, or a coteaching team is reviewing classroom and individual student data. Let's unveil some of the details behind our data mantra …OPA!

ORGANIZING YOUR DATA

You'll organize your data based on the particular questions you are hoping to answer. This organization is done in advance of your meeting. We encourage you to pay attention to how you display the data as well. Be mindful that for many of us a picture is worth a thousand words. Create a graphic display of your data accompanied by a table of numbers. While the questions can become more complex, the essential questions to ask across the continuum of support are listed in Figure 4.5.

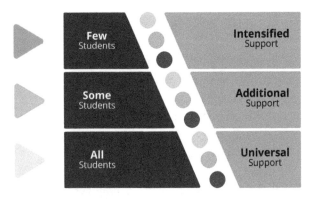

Universal Support

1. What is the academic, behavioral and/or social emotional health of our students? (what percentage is on track?)
2. How are we doing with the big ideas or core competencies of this area of study?
3. Are we doing what we've agreed to be doing with Universal Support (fidelity— what/when/how)?

Additional Support

1. Who may need Additional Support?
2. In what areas/function?
3. Are we doing what we've agreed to be doing with Additional Support (what/when/how)?

Intensified Support

1. For whom is Intensified Support warranted?
2. In what areas/function?
3. For Universal and/or Additional Support?
4. Are we doing what we've agreed to be doing with Intensified Support (what/when/how)?

Source: SWIFT Education Center (2016).

Figure 4.5. **Organizing your data**

PROCESSING YOUR DATA

When processing data, teams who enter in with curiosity and open mindedness and that engage in reflection get the best results. What we mean by this description is that they avoid seeing in the data what they *want* to see and proposing the activities they simply want to do. (We all have inadvertently fallen into this pattern). A data facilitator can play a key role in engaging the teams in the process. Teams are wise to select a facilitator who invites thoughtful decision making. While you want to be efficient, you want to make sure that team members are truly engaging in the process and not just going through the motions. Here are some of our data routine facilitator tips:

1. Check for understanding often.

2. Check for consensus often. You can honor individual perspectives; just be sure to note when a perspective represents "one or some."

3. Be OK with silence. When brainstorming, use the "popcorn is ready" rule. We often explain that, just as when the kernels are popping and they get to the point where there are two to three seconds between pops, you should check to see if the popcorn is done. When there are two to three seconds of silence in a brainstorming session, check to see if more time is needed or if the current observations or idea generation is "done enough" to move on.

4. As a facilitator, avoid participating unless you are a team member as well. The facilitator has an important role in moving the group's discussion and decision making.

ACTING ON YOUR DATA

Now the part that gets energizing! Teams use a data-informed process that moves them from understanding student needs to owning and creating needed learning opportunities. We like to think that this is the part that brings out the best in teams: the amazing expertise and thinking that educators had to do alone before MTSS came along. The key parts of the data-informed process are for teams to

1. identify strengths and needs;

2. home in on a priority focus area;

3. generate ideas; and

4. select resources to support the students.

DATA ROUTINES FOR UNIVERSAL TIER

Engaging in the data routine around the universal tier can be done in a variety of ways (see Figure 4.6). In some settings, school leadership teams review data on a frequent basis (e.g., every two weeks, monthly, every six weeks, quarterly) in order to make adjustments schoolwide. In others, grade-level, department, or professional learning community teams review data that are summarized and supported by the school-level teams. We've even been part of a faculty review of student data that resulted in schoolwide priorities. Through whatever team you deem appropriate, your task at the universal tier is to have a plan to continuously strengthen first instruction in academic, behavioral, and social-emotional domains. Now let's connect the dots with the hard work you've done with your infrastructure.

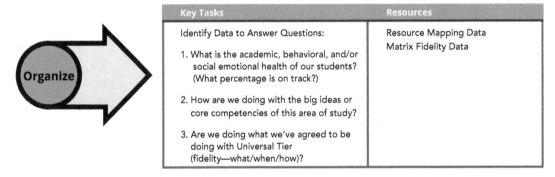

Key Tasks	Resources
Identify Data to Answer Questions: 1. What is the academic, behavioral, and/or social emotional health of our students? (What percentage is on track?) 2. How are we doing with the big ideas or core competencies of this area of study? 3. Are we doing what we've agreed to be doing with Universal Tier (fidelity—what/when/how)?	Resource Mapping Data Matrix Fidelity Data

Source: SWIFT Education Center (2016).

Figure 4.6. **Data sources for universal tier**

FIELD TRiP

ELEMENTARY SCHOOL (K–6)

This example is from a "first-ring" suburban school serving students from kindergarten through sixth grade. This elementary school has a building leadership team, or BLTeam, and utilizes grade-level teams to review academic and behavioral data. The BLTeam summarizes across grade levels the area of focus and a targeted plan to support improvement; it includes grade-level representatives to provide progress updates. Below is how their first-grade team engaged in two parts of the data routine.

Process

The grade-level team included a grade-level teacher, special education teacher, reading specialist, and ELL support provider; it was able to meet for an hour for this process. They were able to make time for the data review while students were in art class and then transitioned to the library by the art teacher. A BLTeam member served as a facilitator for the process so that all other team members could be actively involved in the deep thinking.

Act

The team used a format to capture strengths and needs across multiple data sources to answer their questions (Figure 4.7). Drawing from several data sources, the group recognized that the priority for strengthening needed to be in the area of ensuring mastery and automaticity with phonics and word work. They came to consensus in their discussion, agreeing that they hadn't been consistent with the blending routine for Wonders, providing appropriate practice with the new skills, and had been spending their literacy block time focusing on "getting everything in" from the unit outline instead of ensuring students were "getting it." Meanwhile their data were indicating they needed to firm up students' automaticity with phonics skills. The team used the Wonders unit outline to generate ideas related to addressing phonics during word work time, with an emphasis on active engagement. They discussed how to make time during small-group instruction to do more practice with phonics skills. While they shared a commitment to strengthening phonics instruction, each of the four first-grade teachers determined which ideas would work best with the learners in the individual classrooms.

(Continued)

(Continued)

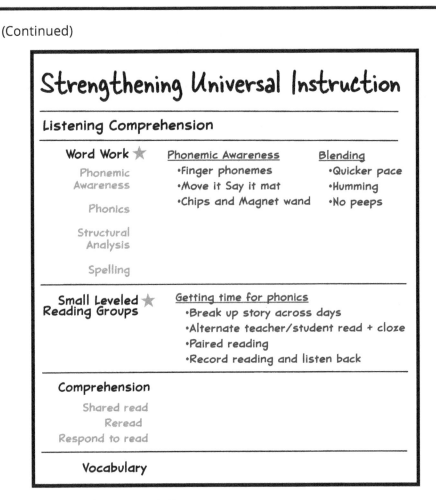

Strengthening Universal Instruction

Listening Comprehension

Word Work ⭐

Phonemic
Awareness

Phonics

Structural
Analysis

Spelling

Phonemic Awareness
•Finger phonemes
•Move it Say it mat
•Chips and Magnet wand

Blending
•Quicker pace
•Humming
•No peeps

Small Leveled ⭐
Reading Groups

Getting time for phonics
•Break up story across days
•Alternate teacher/student read + cloze
•Paired reading
•Record reading and listen back

Comprehension

Shared read
Reread
Respond to read

Vocabulary

Source: SWIFT Education Center (2016).

Figure 4.7. **Data-informed decisions**

What if you don't have a unit outline that will prompt reflection? We're guessing our secondary colleagues had this exact question while reading about this field trip. The elementary school in the previous field trip used the unit outline because this is what they typically planned lessons from. At any grade level, you can think of the decision in relation to lesson plans. How do you approach lesson planning? Do you usually have a fairly predictable format, even it if isn't published? For example, you might always have a part of the lesson that makes explicit linkages to standards and objectives, a part to prime background knowledge, a way to introduce and model skills or concepts, guided practice, independent work, and a resulting demonstration of learning (e.g., product). These lesson plan elements would serve as the parts down the left-hand side of your chart or document, with ideas generated to the right. In fact, here's a secondary field trip.

FIELD TRiP

SECONDARY EXAMPLE

A high school leadership team consisting of all department leads, including the special education lead teacher, decided they would collect more data than required by their district's broad screener for all ninth-grade students. They wondered whether their long list of students with failing grades at semester was related to basic reading skills. The data indicated that of the 515 ninth graders, 75% demonstrated at least one risk factor in reading, with 36% of them demonstrating at least two risk factors in reading. In light of these data, they designed a process to vet recommended reading strategies from the literature that could be taught across all content areas. Before sharing them with staff, each team member tried out the strategy in a class. This approach accomplished two purposes. First, it served as a pilot test to make sure the strategies demonstrated value. Second, this approach allowed the leadership team to share the strategy with their departmental colleagues with specific examples of how it applied in math, social studies, or science. The resulting enhancement menu was captured on a Google document, and corresponding folders allowed staff to add and share related documents (e.g., graphic organizers, student aids, scaffolded assignments) (Figure 4.8). Some staff members created videos of their use of the strategies and added them to the folder. These were appreciated by staff and were highly coveted by teachers new to the school. Brilliant work!

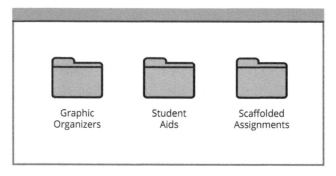

Source: SWIFT Education Center (2016).

Figure 4.8. **Enhancement menu document sharing**

We want to pause here for a moment as we discuss data routines at the universal tier. Think back to the home construction metaphor. What would happen if you moved in and found a slight crack in the foundation, or a leak in your basement? With MTSS, if the universal tier is not comprehensive, appropriate, and responsive, then we run the risk of developing a foundational crack or leak. Many teams come to us asking about how to strengthen their core, that is, their universal tier. We love this question, because it gets right to issues of equity. This question shows that the team is grappling with how to make their "first instruction" strong and reach all of their students. We think of this review of the universal tier as consistent vigilance to make sure the foundation is strong, sturdy, and supportive of a safe and wonderful home. What if your school's foundation lacks the "powerful instructional strategies, differentiation, and universal design for learning" described in Chapter 1 as a foundational element? The data review will begin to show it as a high proportion of students needing additional and/or intensified support.

Here are some questions for your team to ask about whether you need to further strengthen your foundation.

TAKiNG IT TO THE TEAM

STRENGTHENING YOUR FOUNDATION AT THE UNIVERSAL TIER

- Is our universal support designed for every student?

- Do we see evidence that it is having a positive effect on most or all students?

- Is there a demonstrated need for different core instructional materials?

- Are we able to differentiate our instruction effectively within universal support (including time to plan for differentiation)?

- What do we know about student engagement during core instructional periods?

- Can we identify which students universal support is not working for and find a way to address their needs within it?

- Are we able to encourage multiple means of expressions (UDL)?

- Do we feel we have the necessary knowledge around grade-level standards, including what is included in the grade levels above and below the one we teach?

MY THOUGHTS

Now let's jump back to the data routines for resource matching. In this next Taking It To The Team, think about how you organize, process, and act with your data routines related to a universal tier for all students. As we think about matching resources, it is most important to build these supports with broad consensus of their effectiveness.

TAKiNG IT TO THE TEAM

UNIVERSAL DATA-INFORMED DECISION-MAKING ROUTINE

- What teaming structure would make the most sense in our setting for this process?

- Do we have people on the team that understand integrated instruction across academic, behavioral, and social-emotional learning?

- Are there any important truths that we must honor in order to move forward with our data routine to set up the universal tier? (For example, we know we need to pay attention to the performance of particular groups of students, such as students of color, students with disabilities, or other groups that have been historically underserved or low performing in our school.)

- How is this the same or different from the process our school currently uses to act on data?

- Have we established a working team that is not duplicative, but rather one that streamlines workflow for staff to minimize time in meetings?

MY THOUGHTS

DATA ROUTINES ADDITIONAL TIER

What about students who show the need for more support than is available from the universal tier? The data protocol for resource matching for the additional tier is a really amazing experience. Gone are the days when students go down the hall for Title I, special education, or English language support. (If students are still going down the hall in your school, this is a good place to start with your master schedule.) Over time, schools got really good at coordinating around the role of the teacher. If a student had an IEP, then he went to the special education teacher. Eligible for Title I? She went to the Title I teacher. And so on. We understand and appreciate part of the intent of this system was to acknowledge and capitalize on different skill sets and expertise of the teachers and others in the school. You can, however, still do that. In this new structure you can coordinate around collective understanding of each student's needs and matching learning opportunities accordingly. When we talk about the remaking of education with equity at the center, this is the kind of difference we are talking about. We still understand that educators have way too much to do, often with too little support. This common reality is the reason we work to de-silo educational resources and capitalize on collective strengths. We simply will not get where we want to when we organize in a manner that is not related to tiers of intensifying support.

A need-based matching of additional support is distinct in several ways. First, as we've emphasized, matching resources to needs is not based on labels or entitlement. Students don't receive "Title I reading support" in homogeneous groups formed on the basis of low reading scores from a "Title I teacher." Likewise, students who are at risk behaviorally or due to indications of concern related to social-emotional factors aren't homogeneously grouped to receive social skill instruction from the counselor. Rather, teams use screening data from each and every student, create a common understanding of the need, use the matrix to assist with matching needs to support, and make strong and thoughtful matches about who are the best people to meet student needs without segregating or stigmatizing students with seemingly permanent labels. (Don't forget to look back at that group résumé you built.) We are *huge* fans of the notion that we utilize our most highly qualified educators to support students with the most instructional need. Equity-based MTSS and all that it entails may mean that a grade-level teacher or math teacher works with the students who need the most support to understand a particular algebraic concept, while another educator or staff person is facilitating a large-group math activity or lesson with students who are getting enough support from the universal instruction.

Let's put those questions we organize our data around in front of us (Figure 4.9), and then take a trip into a data review process that matched additional support to student needs in math.

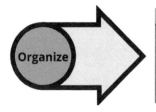

Key Tasks	Resources
Identify Data to Answer Questions: 1. Who may need Additional Support? 2. In what areas/function? 3. Are we doing what we've agreed to be doing with Additional Tier (what/when/how)	Resource Mapping Data Matrix Fidelity Data

Source: SWIFT Education Center (2016).

Figure 4.9. **Organize data for additional tier**

FIELD TRiP

MIDDLE SCHOOL—GRADE 5

Williamston Middle School is a fifth-grade center for the district. The school serves 72 students with four classrooms. The teachers departmentalize core course areas and recently added a 45-minute block to the day to allow for personalized support time. During this block, all staff coordinate small-group or individual instructional arrangements to meet identified needs across all content domains. The arrangements typically can accommodate two 20-minute rotations for support plus 5 minutes for transition, or allow for a longer 45-minute group time, as necessary. Their approach to organizing their data is shown in Figure 4.10.

Key Tasks	Williamston Resources

Identify Data to Answer Questions:
1. Who needs Additional Support?
2. In what areas/function?
3. Are we doing what we've agreed to be doing with Additional Tier (what/when/how)
	Matrix
	Universal Screening Data
	   Acadience reading
	   Acadience math
	   Attendance
	   Student Risk Screening Scale
	   Unit Tests and Formatives

Source: SWIFT Education Center (2016).

Figure 4.10. **Organized data for additional tier in middle school example**

Process

This team facilitates their own process, and each teacher individually reviews student data, validates areas showing concern, and identifies one to two areas that would be good areas of focus during the personalized block over a two-week period. Students also engage in this reflection and share their thoughts with their first-period teacher.

Act

When the team convenes to plan for the two-week personalized block, they individually review their recommendations for who needs what. They depict the needs using sticky notes, so they can get a sense of needs and groupings and discuss possible arrangements during the 45-minute block (Figure 4.11). One of the things that stands out about this team is how carefully they match needs to instruction and support using their matrix. They might have a student with needs in literacy and in fluency, and they can discuss fluency need and known interests of the student, and make decisions with the student about whether Read Naturally, Quick Reads, or a repeated reading routine would make the most effective use of resources. They've been known to be creative in selecting any of the three and even personalizing the selection by having students record their reading on the computer so they can listen back and rate their own fluency, for example. For another student, the team selected Read Naturally over the use of a repeated reading routine, because that student preferred to work independently. This personalization maintains the use of strong evidence-based approaches and allows them to be matched in a way that increases student engagement and likelihood of success.

The team's last planning meeting in this OPA cycle is to determine how the instruction and support will be monitored for fidelity and how progress monitoring will be coordinated. Again, the team uses the matrix for guidance on their progress monitoring tools.

Before launching any changes, they make sure to communicate with both the student and the student's parents or guardians and agree on the direction. This is an active cycle of instruction, and it is important for everyone to have a clear understanding of the goal and support designed to achieve that goal.

(Continued)

(Continued)

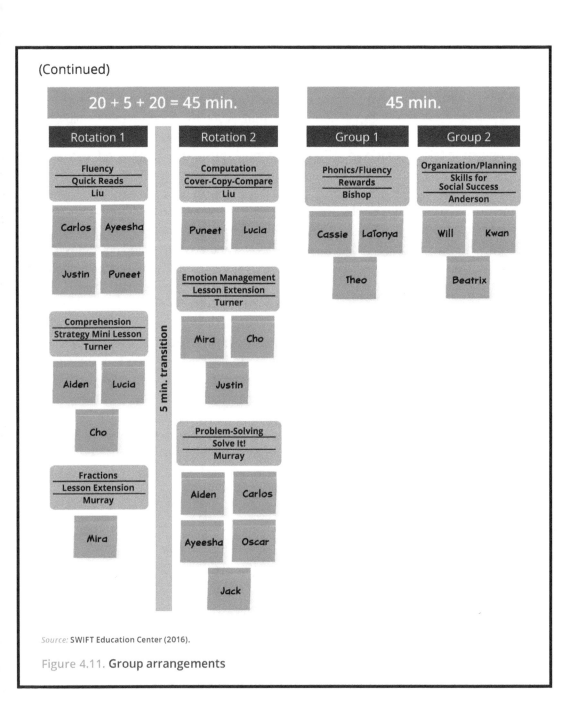

Source: SWIFT Education Center (2016).

Figure 4.11. **Group arrangements**

This data review work may seem like a lot, and quite honestly it is. We do it because we are proactively planning and designing instruction, resources, supports, and a schedule to meet the full array of student needs across academic, behavioral, and social-emotional learning. Yet, as teams continue using this process, they become more efficient, and they begin to function like a well-oiled machine. Educators become fluent at using data routines in support of schoolwide, classwide, and individual student progress. We recently met a high school team that shared their innovative way to make MTSS work was to have content-area classes four days a week, and on Wednesday having a schoolwide flex schedule that allowed for small-group meetings, individual support, peer-study groups, and so on. Imagine how resources could be used with a completely flexible clock to use as needed from week to week!

TAKING IT TO THE TEAM

ADDITIONAL TIER DATA-BASED DECISION-MAKING ROUTINE

- What teaming structure would make the most sense in our setting for this process?

- What could be accomplished with this that would be important for our setting?

- How is this the same as or different from the process our school currently uses to act on data?

- Are all students included in the consideration for additional support? Are all staff considered when matching supports to needs?

- Do we have people on the team who understand integrated instruction across academic, behavioral, and social-emotional learning in the additional tier?

- Are there any important truths that we must honor in order to move forward with our data routine for additional support (e.g., this process is not about sending kids to other places)?

(Continued)

(Continued)

MY THOUGHTS

What about students who have more complex needs? When you have structures that continuously engage you in a discussion that focuses on strengthening the universal tier, *and* you have structures in place that identify needs early, match support accordingly, and monitor progress so you and your team know when a change might be warranted—what does intensified support really mean? The bottom line is that your system has to have a way to know when to "up the ante" and who should be at the table to do that.

As we pointed out with the additional tier, the intensified tier is not people and places separated from the whole. It is about deeply understanding and bringing a planning process to the table centered on universal and additional tier efforts. Common missteps at that this level include setting up time blocks for "interventions" with assigned content within your master schedule without matching that to a specific learning need; or selecting an individual to provide additional or intensified support who is responsible for progress or growth of the students, but not clearly predetermining the content and resources or not including them in the resource-matching process. We want to set up a system so that educators don't have to make one up repeatedly. Of course, we still want to be sure to continue to group students based on their instructional needs, not any other variable (equity check here again). Then lastly, and this one can be tricky particularly at middle and high school, we want to be sure all educators know of and understand the menu of support resources (see the tiered instructional matrix) and how the various resources are specifically applied to student needs based on data.

The goal is to figure out what is needed for an individual student to make *progress* in identified areas. The good news is that the people in the system who have been engaging in these routines will just be drilling down and getting more precise and intentional about the planning for an individual student—*not* going in a different direction. This continuity creates a well-understood, formal system of support for each and every student that is part of a larger system of support (Figure 4.12).

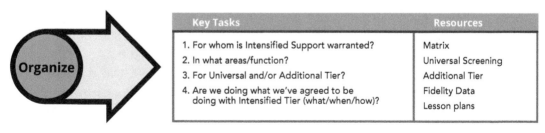

Key Tasks	Resources
1. For whom is Intensified Support warranted? 2. In what areas/function? 3. For Universal and/or Additional Tier? 4. Are we doing what we've agreed to be doing with Intensified Tier (what/when/how)?	Matrix Universal Screening Additional Tier Fidelity Data Lesson plans

Source: SWIFT Education Center (2016).

Figure 4.12. **Organize data for intensified tier**

As we look at the questions that will help organize your data, the only key difference between them and the questions you asked in the additional tier process is whether or not the planning needs to address the universal tier or the additional tier or both. Let's take a look at what this process looks like in an early childhood setting (Figure 4.13).

FIELD TRiP

EARLY LEARNING CENTER

The early learning center (ELC) is part of a mid-size district on the outskirts of a southern metro area. The ELC serves three- and four-year-old students with two or more district-identified risk factors. The ELC has been building an integrated academic and behavioral MTSS for several years.

Key Tasks	Early Learning Center Resources
Identify Data to Answer Questions: 1. Who needs Additional Support? 2. In what areas/function? 3. Are we doing what we've agreed to be doing with Additional Tier (what/when/how)?	Matrix Universal Screening Data Progress Monitoring Data Fidelity Reflection

Source: SWIFT Education Center (2016).

Figure 4.13. **Organized data for intensified tier in early childhood center example**

Process

The ELC has teaming structures that include a center leadership team that meets monthly to review center data and work on strengthening their system, and age-based teams consisting of classroom teachers and aides who meet weekly to review classwide and individual student data. When a team is not sure about changes that should be made or when others may be involved in the support plan, they invite those individuals to the table too. While families receive daily communication about their child, team members work to make sure families are involved in individual student planning. If they cannot attend in person, staff engage them

---

by phone or email to be sure their voices are included in the process. Typically, individual student planning teams ask a colleague who is less involved with the student to facilitate so that the team can be fully engaged in thinking.

Act

When the team finds that a change is warranted, they determine the scope of intensification and use the checklist depicted in Figure 4.14 to launch their thinking about ways in which intensifying might be done to increase success of their efforts. The example provided illustrates a team that included the child's family. They were working to increase this child's ability to follow directions by teaching him to use strategies when frustrated, and to improve his successful playing with peers in center time. Universal support included such practices as visual prompts and reminders, practice, positive feedback, and consistent use of routines and rituals. At first his additional support included small-group mini lessons focused on following directions, and using "Sophie" books to reinforce self-regulation.

After the team processed what had been working and what they were learning about the child, they generated different ideas about ways to intensify both universal and additional support. The ideas they highlighted on the checklist were those that the teacher and family thought had a strong likelihood of working. They built off those universal and additional supports that were well matched to his needs, and intensified the supports by (a) having the counselor meet with him for 10 minutes at the beginning of each day to do a self-regulation game that was more kinesthetic in nature (e.g., Stop and Go game) and to practice one of the Conscious Discipline skills (e.g., deep breathing with the Hoberman sphere ball); (b) sending home a Sophie book to be read with an extension activity that he could do with a parent, which would reinforce the skill focus of the book; and (c) having a one-on-one debrief at the end of the day with either the teacher or counselor. The other ideas generated were kept on record in case the team needed to come back to them. Before they concluded the meeting, they determined a reasonable timeline for reconvening, indicated on the progress monitoring chart when they made these changes, and verified a communication plan that would work among them to sharing progress reports.

(Continued)

(Continued)

Early Childhood MTSS   Checklist for Intensifying Universal and Additional Support

Date:	Teacher:	Observer/Coach (if applicable):	

General Area (Reading, Math, Behavior, Language, Other):			

Skill Area Being Targeted: Self regulation

Specific Skill to Target: Following directions and emotion management

Intensifying Universal Support and Intervention		
Grouping	**Y/N/NA**	**Notes or Next Steps (If Applicable)**
Can small, flexible groups be used diferently? Or individual learning opportunities be provided?	⭐	–Meet with teacher or counselor begining and end of day
Can peer model be used differently?		–Change circle seating arrangements
Can groups/centers be more appropriately matched to student need?		–Social story using classroom schedule with emphasis on following directions
Instruction		
Can small, flexible groups be used diferently? Or individual learning opportunities be provided?	⭐	–Make self regulation games kinesthetic (e.g., Stop & Go game) –Combine Hoberman's sphere ball with breathing exercise
Can peer model be used differently?		
Do we need to break the tasks or skills down into smaller parts?		
Do we need to teach any pre-skills?		
Can we make changes to our modeling and opportunities for practice?	⭐	–More practice with Conscious Discipline skills (e.g., Deep Breathing, relationship) He loves the "Balloon & Drain" –Role play after reading Sophie books
Do we need to change instruction to demonstrate culturally responsive practices?		
Feedback		
Can we enhance the immediate, positive feedback that is provided?		–Loves emoji stickers
Would self-monitoring strategies make sense?		–Add visual timer –Add self graphing using sticker chart
Frequency and Duration		
Can we change the frequency of the instruction or support?	⭐	–Daily 1:1 time
Can we change the duration of the instruction or support?		
Other Considerations		
Can we provide opportunities for families to engage in instruction?	⭐	–Send home Sophie books w/ home activities –Coordinate with mom and dad
Can we better communicate progress to family(ies)?		–Daily positive email that can be reinforced at home
Have we learned anything about the child from the family that should be considered?		
Could additional support be provided to family(ies) to engage in targeted skill instruction?		

Source: SWIFT Education Center (2016).

Figure 4.14. Data-informed decision-making checklist, early childhood center example

TAKiNG IT TO THE TEAM

INTENSIFIED TIER DATA-BASED DECISION-MAKING ROUTINE

- (For early childhood settings) Have we considered this level of organized support in our setting?

- (For elementary schools) Do we have a team structure in place that allows intensifying universal and/or additional support as suggested?

- (For middle and high schools) How might intensification occur in content-specific classes? How might student involvement be different at the secondary level?

- What teaming structure would make the most sense for this process in our setting?

- What could be accomplished with this tier that would be important for our students?

- How is this tier the same as or different from the process our school currently uses for individual planning?

MY THOUGHTS

CONTINUOUSLY IMPROVING YOUR MTSS

Always have a plan and believe in it. Nothing happens by accident.

—CHUCK KNOX (N.D.)

Okay, now to the honey-do list that we referenced in the opening paragraphs of this chapter (Figure 4.15). We hope that up to this point you are recognizing how many components and practices you already have related to equity-based MTSS that you can shift, reorganize, or repurpose to meet the needs of all students. As you've been going through this journey, you may have been keeping track of things you want or want to do.

To Do List

1. Screener addressing social emotional needs
2. Stronger math profile for students not taking written assessment
3. Additional support that will address students needing organization and self-regulation skills
4. Universal instructional practices framework
5. Vetted resources for informational text across all grade levels
6. Explore co-teaching
7. Schedule vertical teaming time

Source: SWIFT Education Center (2016).

Figure 4.15. **Honey-do list for MTSS**

Your list may be longer than the one we show here. Long lists are usually the case! You know that we started by focusing you on what you *do* have, because equity is too important to wait for the perfect conditions to arrive. But we know it is healthy to recognize what you want and to strive for those better conditions. Remember those TA practices we introduced in Chapter 1? While they help you move through a transformation, they also support continuous improvement. We want to make sure you have enough insight into one of these practices that is particularly important for, well, let's call it home improvement!

We want to zero in on the "priorities" TA practice to help you begin to work on your to-do list. If you recall, this practice relies on stage-based planning concepts that increase the probability that those things you want for your system will be (1) based on strong decisions, (2) properly planned, (3) implemented by well-prepared and confident people, and (4) monitored closely by you to make sure they're working for staff and students alike. We aren't finance people, but we know enough to suggest that you are more likely to get a return on your investment if you approach "what's next" in this way.

First, let us say that what we are sharing here first requires you to prioritize the honey-do list. It isn't financially reasonable or humanly possible to take on the entire list. We know educators have superpowers, but there is a limit to being able to take on new practices and maintain daily professional practices at a high level. This process takes three to five years (bummer), but remember, we are transforming education here. This list is the start of moving down that path. When you make a decision about what it is you want or need, let's just use the first one on the list—*selecting a screener*—that will give you a snapshot of the health of your system and identify students who many need additional support with behavioral or social-emotional skills. The priorities practice tool is going to help your team purposefully select practices that will serve your need, and the tool will engage your team in thoughtful and intentional planning. Trust us, you're really going to love this! This is our favorite TA practice.

The priorities practice is based on the work of the National Implementation Research Network (NIRN) referenced in an earlier chapter. Once you have a practice that you want to install in your school, like a universal screener addressing behavioral and social-emotional needs, your team can use the following tool to determine an entry point for planning (Figure 4.16).

PRiORITIES STAGE-BASED IMPLEMENTATION

Priority: An opportunity identified by the team in order to achieve their vision.

Practice: A purposefully selected intervention or collection of activities that leads to accomplishment of a priority.

Laying the Foundation Why/What?	Installing Where/How?	Implementing How are we learning?	Sustaining Schoolwide Implementation How are we sustaining?
Learn Options	Prepare People & Systems	Try Out the Practice	Students & System Outcomes show the Practice Works
Choose Practice	Train	Reflect & Recommend Improvements in Practice & System	Competent, Organized, Well-Led Systems for Practice

1. We know what options (practices) exist for this priority.

2. We agree on which practice we want to implement.

3. We have people and systems prepared to implement this practice.

4. We have well-trained people who will be trying-out this practice.

5. We have tried out this practice.

6. We have reflected on initial implementation efforts and recommended improvements in the practice and systems that support it.

7. We have student and system outcomes that show this practice is working.

8. We have a competent, organized, well-led system for this practice.

Source: SWIFT Education Center (2016).

Figure 4.16. **Priorities practice tool**

The first stage, laying the foundation, guides teams to learn about options that exist and to make choices that are a good fit for their system. The second stage is that of installing. Installing makes sure that you prepare the people and systems for the practices you want to put in place. You want to ensure that your people understand the what, why, and how of the practices (*how*, we might note, is often the most underappreciated aspect of them all). Once the people are confident and well prepared to put the practice in place, planning turns attention to implementing, monitoring, and making sure supports are adequate and outcomes are positive. The last stage is that of sustaining implementation. So often we let something new turn our attention from finishing the work. You need to make sure your team pays attention, nurtures, and continues to support those finishing touches on your equity-based MTSS.

MY THOUGHTS

Here's how the process works. Basically, you'll ask the questions that are numbered and stop where your team answers "no." Since we've set you up with things on your list that you don't have—yet—you will likely be stopping with Question 1 or Question 2. What are the implications? Here's part two of the priorities tools—specific prompts that will engage your team in deep and meaningful planning (Figure 4.17).

PRiORITIES

School/District:

Priority: Practice:

Laying the Foundation: Stage-Based Outcomes

1) We know what options (practices) exist for this priority.
- ☐ We are able to identify practices that would be associated with our priority.
- ☐ We know what options exist to address our priority.

2) We agree on which practice we want to implement.
- ☐ We have a clear (enough) description of what this practice will look like in our school/district.
- ☐ We are clear on who will be involved in selecting the practice we want to implement.
- ☐ We are clear (enough) on WHO will be doing WHAT, WHERE, and the CONDITIONS (when/how).
- ☐ Key stakeholders agree with the rationale for and descriptions of the practice.

Installing: Stage-Based Outcomes

3) We have people and systems prepared to implement this practice.
- ☐ We have described where and with whom we will be implementing.
- ☐ We have identified structural or functional changes needed to implement the practice (e.g. staffing, scheduling, responsibilities).
- ☐ We have brainstormed possible barriers, or things that might limit the success of our implementation, to inform our planning.
- ☐ People know where to go with questions about implementation.
- ☐ People know how to document challenges and successes with implementation and know how that information will be used.
- ☐ If we are doing a pilot, our School/District Leadership Teams know when implementation starts and ends.
- ☐ School/District Leadership Teams know how they will:
    — Promote positive messages about implementation to stakeholders
    — Evaluate implementation (fidelity, satisfaction, outcomes)
- ☐ Leaders know how the results will inform decisions to revise, continue, expand, or discontinue implementation.

4) We have well-trained people who will be trying out this practice.
- ☐ We have allocated the training resources and planned out the training logistics.
- ☐ Those who will be implementing are well trained.
- ☐ We have evidence showing that those who will be implementing the practice have the basic knowledge and skills they need.
- ☐ We have coaching and support available for people who are implementing the practice.
- ☐ We have a clear and common understanding of what implementation of this practice looks like.

Source: SWIFT Education Center (2016).

Figure 4.17. **Priorities practice checklist**

PRiORITIES

Implementing: Stage-Based Outcomes

5) We have tried out this practice. We are trying out this practice.
- ☐ We are capturing the essential information about how implementation is going, including facilitators and barriers.
- ☐ Our leadership teams are promoting this practice.
- ☐ We know whether or not we are doing this practice the way it was intended.
- ☐ Those trying out the practice are well coached. They feel competent using the practice.
- ☐ We are getting (some of) the desired outcomes.
- ☐ We are communicating with all stakeholders about implementing this practice.

6) We have reflected on initial implementation efforts and recommended improvements to support the practice and systems.
- ☐ We have examined all the essential aspects of the system relative to this practice (Drivers Best Practices).

  Based on what we are learning:
- ☐ We are enhancing the competency of our people.
- ☐ We are enhancing our organizational capacity to use this practice.
- ☐ We are enhancing how we capture desired outcomes for students and the system.
- ☐ We are enhancing how we lead the use of this practice.
- ☐ The school and district administrative policies and practices sufficiently support this practice.

Sustaining Schoolwide Implementation: Stage-Based Outcomes

7) We have student and system outcomes that show this practice is working.
- ☐ We can demonstrate the student outcomes directly related to using this practice.
- ☐ We can demonstrate the system outcomes directly related to using this practice.

8) We have a competent, organized, well-led system for this practice.
- ☐ Our leadership teams are using outcome, fidelity, and satisfaction data to make decisions about this practice.
- ☐ Our feedback processes are in place and functional (within and across all arenas: school, district, community).
- ☐ We can demonstrate a competent, organized, and well-led system for this practice (e.g., we have essential components IN PLACE as documented by the Drivers Best Practices tool).
- ☐ We are continuously improving and aligning this practice within our system.

Source: SWIFT Education Center (2016).

We recognize this is a lot of information. Why not just go down the honey-do list and get it done? It's really comes back to how we prepare our people and the system. Gone are the days of going straight to implementation of the next thing that shows up on the district's professional development calendar. The frame of equity-based MTSS requires thoughtful, purposeful, and planned supports. The rationale behind it is that we change the way we implement practices based on our priorities so that those practices actually stick around. When implementing practices schoolwide, we don't want to make that decision lightly, because it requires the energy of the whole system. Have you ever worked for a leader who has wanted to take on everything (or have you ever been that leader)? It makes the lift just too heavy. We suggest this priorities tool as a way to protect your investment in equity-based MTSS and allow only thoughtfully planned practices to enter when the system is ready. The planning form below can be used for that purpose (Figure 4.18).

PRiORITIES PLANNING FORM

Priority	
Practice	

Action Step	Who	By When	Status Update / Next Steps
Laying the Foundation			
Installing			
Implementing			
Sustaining Schoolwide Implementation			

Source: SWIFT Education Center (2016).

Figure 4.18. Priorities planning form

Let's take a look at another field trip so you can see what this looks like in action.

FIELD TRiP

PRIORITIES PLANNING

A middle school located in a remote rural district took on the issue of identifying screeners that would help them know which students might need more support for behavioral and social-emotional learning. They had a very strong academic assessment and instruction system in place and were seeking to make sure they had the counterpart behavioral and social-emotional systems to meet their small, albeit complex, student body needs. They had made headway with some universal behavior systems, namely setting and teaching schoolwide expectations and establishing a reliable office discipline referral system. Working with their regional system for PBIS support, they wanted to make sure their assessment system was more comprehensive.

They utilized the tools we provided to take "two steps back to take them four steps forward." As depicted in the following plan (Figure 4.19), they first recognized that they wanted to know more about options that existed—not just by name. First, they identified what was important to them, that is, what criteria a good screening tool would meet. In addition, they wanted to explore what tools were recommended by groups doing research on behalf of the department of education. And they had a team member share what they learned about the NIRN "hexagon tool," which helps organize all this exploratory information in a way that helps the team make decisions.

This planning process made the team rightfully confident, not only about the decision they made, but also in how they could transparently explain the selection process to all the stakeholders who had a vested interest in the outcome. They were able to select a screener; answering the questions on the priorities tool, they decided to pilot the tool in third grade before schoolwide implementation. This set them up to really prepare the people and the system for the next step in their MTSS process.

PRiORITIES PLANNING FORM

Priority	Inclusive Behavior Instruction — Data-informed decision making
Practice	Screening for behavior/social emotional indicators of need

Action Step	Who	By When	Status Update / Next Steps
Laying the Foundation			
1. Identifying criteria important to us 2. Research questions to ask CDE 3. Hexagon tool overview for group	1. Team 2. Dave 3. Verneda	Next Meeting	
Installing			
Implementing			
Sustaining Schoolwide Implementation			

Source: SWIFT Education Center (2016).

Figure 4.19. **Priorities planning example**

The honey-do list really becomes a lot more than a to-do list. It becomes the way in which the team members implement what they want, when they want, and how they want. These to-dos evolve over time as you continue to make a house your home. As teams begin to really understand this complex, multifunctional system of support, it simply becomes the way teaching and learning get done. You have less fear about how things are going to be, because you and your colleagues understand and can predict the process for change within the MTSS. This honey-do list eventually makes its way into your school improvement plans and local control plans. These priorities become *the plan,* so time is not invested each year trying to figure out where you are going, because you already know where—you simply make the next improvement or modification. The nice part is the direction you are going is evidence based, sure to result in improved outcomes for all student groups. It is really something that can be implemented, not just goals that were written because the plan had to be done (guilty of that once or twice over here ☺).

Ready for another field trip? Meet James, another champion educator/principal we have the privilege of knowing. He inspires us with his ability to transform his school and generously share his leadership skills with educators across his state. His school's student outcome data continued to rise over several years—above the 95% benchmark for early grades—at the same time the proportions of students learning English as an additional language and of students who received free and reduced-price meals rose. His is a story worth telling!

FIELD TRiP

JAMES'S WHY MTSS

From the very beginning of my work with students, I have found it necessary to find ways to be innovative and creative to meet the needs of individual and groups of students. As one of those few educators that school was never particularly easy for, or interesting, I quickly became aware as a young teacher that school didn't really work for all children. Some kids are adrift in problematic issues happening in their lives, some just don't like the structure of school and are left wanting a creative outlet, and some just aren't able to make sense of what their teachers are trying to get across to them in their daily lessons. What was even more perplexing to me, as I looked at the gifts of many students, was that school has, oftentimes, little to do with the intellect of the child. I saw early on that the culture and expectations of the school and school district, and the willingness of the educators to ensure student success, is a major factor on whether a child succeeds academically, socially, and emotionally. Ultimately, it comes down to the relationship and trust that the teachers have cultivated in students and the willingness of the teachers to meet the needs of *all* of their students.

When I think of the opportunity to change the old structures of schools and create a multi-tiered system of support that is meant to meet the needs of *all* students, I get very motivated. Meeting the social-emotional needs of students ensures that they are able to access academic support with success. Student interests and talents are major elements to enable interest and growth in nurturing a productive child into adulthood. It is essential that school systems create the opportunity to arrange curriculum, instruction, and assessment of content while training educators, through ongoing professional development, to create a system where leaders, teachers, students, parents, and community create a culture to empower all learners to succeed.

With that, all stakeholders have to agree on their moral purpose, and ultimately on what—as a team of educators, students, parents, and the educational system—they are endeavoring to achieve. A MTSS is essential to lead members of the educational community, along with the students and their support system, to a place where they can achieve collective efficacy for the success of *all* students. Creating a MTSS is a meaningful avenue to create collective efficacy so that system can truly meet the multiple needs and desires of the students we serve.

CONCLUSION
EQUITY-BASED MTSS—A REALITY!

 I believe that to meet the challenges of our time, human beings will have to develop a great sense of universal responsibility. Each of us must learn to work not just for oneself, one's own family or nation, but for the benefit of all humankind. Universal responsibility is the key to human survival.

—THE DALAI LAMA (AS QUOTED IN CLOKE & HECKMAN, 2018)

We have no doubt that some of the hardest-working individuals in our country are educators. Every year educators are asked to do more with less for our nation's children. As the needs of students grow, we simply must change how we do education. We can no longer effectively teach under the current demands. For many years, we educators, in order to survive the barrage of educational initiatives, sometimes closed our doors and did our very best to teach our students while letting the *current initiative* float on by. There is no shame in this approach (we must admit, we too are guilty of this one), but equity-based MTSS is different. It is not an educational initiative that erases our collective past professional efforts; rather it embraces them.

Equity-based MTSS lets us take all that *is* working in our system and harness it and grow it. It celebrates the strengths and talents of the people in the system and honors what they bring to the table—their histories, cultures, and teaching skills. Equity-based MTSS lays a lasting foundation from which our students are each recognized and supported.

When we are able to

- identify our "why,"
- understand the "what" of equity-based MTSS, and
- learn "how" to put it into practice,

then, we have the blueprint for success for our new home, or in this case our new school. We can fundamentally change our schools. On this strong foundation we encourage you in equipping your educators, utilizing the processes and tools we shared with you. You have the ability to truly transform your systems to reach each one of your students and make a difference in their lives, their families, and the community you are in together.

TAKiNG IT TO THE TEAM

ONE MORE TIME

- Remember that list you made in the Introduction? Did we get there?

- Did we put in motion a structure that would truly support each and every student?

- Did we think about support in a way that would make our jobs as educators more efficient?

- Did we rethink how we meet student need—for each and every student?

MY THOUGHTS

EQUiTY REPORT CARD

- [ ] We as a staff believe in "all means all" and that each and every child should have a place in our school that is not segregated in any way.

- [ ] I as an individual recognize that all children can learn and that I have an active role in their learning.

- [ ] I individually and we collectively actively examine whether all student groups represented in our community are a part of our school. We ask ourselves, "Who is missing?"

- [ ] Staff who serve my school embrace the mindset that each child can learn to high levels.

- [ ] Staff who serve my school have a shared understanding of our collective resources.

- [ ] Staff understand that we will consider all resources as we understand student needs.

- [ ] We have shifted our thinking from "yours" and "mine" to "ours."

- [ ] We have articulated the expectations of what Universal, Additional, and Intensified tiers are inclusive of all learners.

- [ ] We have screening and progress monitoring tools that will help guide decisions across academic, behavior, and social-emotional learning domains that are inclusive of all learners. Our tools are technically sound to the maximum extent available.

- [ ] We approach the creation of a student-centered master schedule by considering time, people, and spaces as variables we can alter to impact changes in student outcomes.

- [ ] We are committed to working with the master schedule in a dynamic manner, meaning that we make adjustments based on student data and a clear understanding of our design, needs, current reality, and strengths.

- [ ] Our resulting master schedule reflects our beliefs, attitudes, values, and priorities.

- [ ] We are prepared to continuously improve our system, reflecting on the data, available resources, and our shared values.

- [ ] We understand the value of social-emotional learning as a mechanism for building equitable support.

☐ We commit to regularly revisit our thinking around equity as we learn more about the historical pain of many and the incredible pride and individual humanity of each child and his or her family.

☐ We commit to learning the names of all our students, our coworkers, and their families.

☐ We celebrate all the family structures that make up our student and school population.

☐ We recognize that equity demands that we do more, even though we have already given so much.

☐ We recognize that throughout our careers we must challenge ourselves to deeply understand the students who come to us, and we commit to changing our practices as part of the way we do business.

☐ We work in a place where we know we have a voice, we belong, and we work daily to show others belong too.

☐ We see evidence of authentic student and family voice in our school community.

☐ We recognize and commit to MTSS as the framework for building equity in our school, and we support the time investment it will require over a number of years.

☐ We recognize that, no matter how long we have been working on equity, in many ways we are still just beginning.

☐ We recognize that we are educators, and we are quite simply amazing. ☺

Source: SWIFT Education Center (2016).

Figure 4.21. **Equity report card**

We promised at the start of this book that you would get a report card, an equity report card. We wanted to pull this out as an additional way to understand equity. Your team could start with it, if they wanted, prior to engaging in the whole transformation process. Use it where and when it works for you and your team (Figures 4.20 and 4.21).

There you have it. Did we make you feel as if you could change the world? Wait …you already do. Thank you for reading our book, for investing your professional lives in the well-being and success of students. We hope we have helped you find a pathway for entering into equity-based MTSS, and that this journey lands us all in a place where our schools are buildings filled with optimism, a sense of community, and success for students, their families, educators, and the communities where we live.

Here is one more field trip you don't want to miss: Dawn's why.

FIELD TRiP

DAWN'S WHY MTSS

I've reflected on my "why" for MTSS often through my work with different schools, districts, and states. Each time I share this exercise with a group, I can't help but do my own reflection. Interestingly, my why has many angles, sometimes because I am thinking about my own children experiencing the journey of school, sometimes because of memories I have when I find a picture that I snapped—a picture of a meeting facilitated on a white board, and sometimes when I hear of a situation with a partner site that takes me back to a familiar place and time.

Over the course of my career, I have had the opportunity to work in and with more than one hundred districts. As I have become part of their processes, I greatly appreciate the spotlight they shine on groups of students they have been most concerned about. For some, it was recognizing and grappling with making their system stronger for students with disabilities—especially those with the most extensive support needs. For others, it was questioning and determining how to address the needs of students who are chronically absent, many of whom included students experiencing anxiety, bullying, and dealing with past trauma. In some places, it was owning and understanding implicit bias that was affecting relationships and experiences of students of color. I appreciate that we go to vulnerable places as we address these situations—being vulnerable individually and being vulnerable and humble with each other as we seek to make our systems stronger. One more thing we have in common is the belief that we have among us the ability to make systems work—make them ready for the next child who enters through our doors. No matter.

Early in my career, I was blessed to have as colleagues, mentors, and friends two amazing individuals: Dr. Jeff Grimes and Dr. David Tilly. I will never forget a keynote they gave at an MTSS Innovations conference about 19 years ago. They titled it "On the Backs of Giants, in the Hands of Wizards." This title serves as a summary of my why. In the keynote, they drew attention to the giants—those researchers who sought answers to "what works and what's needed." For me, these were important giants like Ken Howell, Stan Deno, Jim Ysseldyke, Janet Graden, George Batsche, Zig Englemann, Wes Becker, and of course, Wayne Sailor.

When Jeff and Dave talked about "in the hands of wizards," they showed the clip from *Harry Potter* where Hagrid sought out Harry to tell him that he is a wizard. Harry replied, "You've made a mistake. I can't be a wizard—I'm just Harry."

We are the wizards. You are the wizards. We benefit from those who have put evidence-based practices in our hands. It is up to us to never doubt that we can figure out how to make it work in our system—we have to dig deep, lean on each other, and maintain focus on what matters. We've got this.

APPENDIX
BLANK FORMS

RESOURCE MAPPING

Resource & Intention	Task	Example
Personnel		
Facilities		
Curriculum, Instruction & Supports		
Time Allocations & Requirements		
Data Sources		
Additional Resources		

Source: SWIFT Education Center (2016).

TIERED INSTRUCTION MATRIX

School/District: Grade(s):   Date:

Curricular Area: ☐ Literacy   ☐ Mathmatics   ☐ Behavior/Social Emotional Learning

Part 1: Universal Support	
What	
When	

Part 2: Universal Screening			
Tools	Who Administers		When Administered
	Additional Support		Intensified Support
	...to meet benchmark	...when exceeding benchmark	...to meet benchmark	...when exceeding benchmark
Decision Rules	if...then	if...then	if...then	if...then

Part 3: Instruction and Support			
	Who Provides		When Provided
	Additional Support		Intensified Support
Area identified for support	...to meet benchmark	...when exceeding benchmark	options to consider
Skill Area			

Part 4: Progress Monitoring			
Tools	Who Administers		When Administered
	Additional Support		Intensified Support
	...to meet benchmark	...when exceeding benchmark	...to meet benchmark	...when exceeding benchmark
Decision Rules	if...then	if...then	if...then	if...then

Source: SWIFT Education Center (2016).

MASTER SCHEDULE

(School Year)

Day of the Week

	8:50	9:00	9:30	10:00	10:30	11:00	11:30	12:00	12:30	1:00	1:30	2:00	2:30	3:10
Teacher 1														Dismissal
Teacher 2					Kindergarten									Dismissal
Teacher 1														Dismissal
Teacher 2					Grade 1									Dismissal
Teacher 1														Dismissal
Teacher 2					Grade 2									Dismissal
Teacher 1														Dismissal
Teacher 2					Grade 3									Dismissal
Teacher 1														Dismissal
Teacher 2					Grade 4									Dismissal
Teacher 1														Dismissal
Teacher 2					Grade 5									Dismissal
				Specialized Educators, Related Service Providers, and Support Staff										
Specialized Educators														
Support Staff														Dismissal
Related Service Providers														

Source: SWIFT Education Center (2016).

RESOURCE MATCHING

School/District: _____   Grade(s): _____   Date: _____

Curricular Area: ☐ Literacy ☐ Mathmatics ☐ Behavior/Social Emotional Learning

Area of Need	Student Group	Instructor	Time	Location
Phonics				
Phonemic Awareness				
Vocabulary				

- Area of Need and Student Groups are identified by screening, progress monitoring, or previous assessment; available interventions are located on the Tiered Instruction Matrix.

- N/A means Not Applicable, means no current needs identified by data.

- Instructor, Time, and Location are the available personnel, time, and space located on the Resource Inventory and Master Schedule.

Source: SWIFT Education Center (2016).

PRiORITIES

Priority: Practice:

Laying the Foundation: Stage-Based Outcomes

1) We know what options (practices) exist for this priority.
- ☐ We are able to identify practices that would be associated with our priority.
- ☐ We know what options exist to address our priority.

2) We agree on which practice we want to implement.
- ☐ We have a clear (enough) description of what this practice will look like in our school/district.
- ☐ We are clear on who will be involved in selecting the practice we want to implement.
- ☐ We are clear (enough) on WHO will be doing WHAT, WHERE, and the CONDITIONS (when/how).
- ☐ Key stakeholders agree with the rationale for and descriptions of the practice.

Installing: Stage-Based Outcomes

3) We have people and systems prepared to implement this practice.
- ☐ We have described where and with whom we will be implementing.
- ☐ We have identified structural or functional changes needed to implement the practice (e.g. staffing, scheduling, responsibilities).
- ☐ We have brainstormed possible barriers, or things that might limit the success of our implementation, to inform our planning.
- ☐ People know where to go with questions about implementation.
- ☐ People know how to document challenges and successes with implementation and know how that information will be used.
- ☐ If we are doing a pilot, our School/District Leadership Teams know when implementation starts and ends.
- ☐ School/District Leadership Teams know how they will:
    — Promote positive messages about implementation to stakeholders
    — Evaluate implementation (fidelity, satisfaction, outcomes)
- ☐ Leaders know how the results will inform decisions to revise, continue, expand, or discontinue implementation.

4) We have well-trained people who will be trying out this practice.
- ☐ We have allocated the training resources and planned out the training logistics.
- ☐ Those who will be implementing are well trained.
- ☐ We have evidence showing that those who will be implementing the practice have the basic knowledge and skills they need.
- ☐ We have coaching and support available for people who are implementing the practice.
- ☐ We have a clear and common understanding of what implementation of this practice looks like.

(Continued)

PRiORITIES

Continued

Implementing: Stage-Based Outcomes

5) We have tried out this practice. We are trying out this practice.
- ☐ We are capturing the essential information about how implementation is going, including facilitators and barriers.
- ☐ Our leadership teams are promoting this practice.
- ☐ We know whether or not we are doing this practice the way it was intended.
- ☐ Those trying out the practice are well coached. They feel competent using the practice.
- ☐ We are getting (some of) the desired outcomes.
- ☐ We are communicating with all stakeholders about implementing this practice.

6) We have reflected on initial implementation efforts and recommended improvements to support the practice and systems.
- ☐ We have examined all the essential aspects of the system relative to this practice (Drivers Best Practices).

Based on what we are learning:
- ☐ We are enhancing the competency of our people.
- ☐ We are enhancing our organizational capacity to use this practice.
- ☐ We are enhancing how we capture desired outcomes for students and the system.
- ☐ We are enhancing how we lead the use of this practice.
- ☐ The school and district administrative policies and practices sufficiently support this practice.

Sustaining Schoolwide Implementation: Stage-Based Outcomes

7) We have student and system outcomes that show this practice is working.
- ☐ We can demonstrate the student outcomes directly related to using this practice.
- ☐ We can demonstrate the system outcomes directly related to using this practice.

8) We have a competent, organized, well-led system for this practice.
- ☐ Our leadership teams are using outcome, fidelity, and satisfaction data to make decisions about this practice.
- ☐ Our feedback processes are in place and functional (within and across all arenas: school, district, community).
- ☐ We can demonstrate a competent, organized, and well-led system for this practice (e.g., we have essential components IN PLACE as documented by the Drivers Best Practices tool).
- ☐ We are continuously improving and aligning this practice within our system.

Source: SWIFT Education Center (2016).

PRiORITIES PLANNING FORM

Priority	
Practice	

Action Step	Who	By When	Status Update / Next Steps
Laying the Foundation			
Installing			
Implementing			
Sustaining Schoolwide Implementation			

Source: SWIFT Education Center (2016).

EQUİTY REPORT CARD

- ☐ We as a staff believe in "all means all" and that each and every child should have a place in our school that is not segregated in any way.

- ☐ I as an individual recognize that all children can learn and that I have an active role in their learning.

- ☐ I individually and we collectively actively examine whether all student groups represented in our community are a part of our school. We ask ourselves, "Who is missing?"

- ☐ Staff who serve my school embrace the mindset that each child can learn to high levels.

- ☐ Staff who serve my school have a shared understanding of our collective resources.

- ☐ Staff understand that we will consider all resources as we understand student needs.

- ☐ We have shifted our thinking from "yours" and "mine" to "ours."

- ☐ We have articulated the expectations of what Universal, Additional, and Intensified tiers are inclusive of all learners.

- ☐ We have screening and progress monitoring tools that will help guide decisions across academic, behavior, and social-emotional learning domains that are inclusive of all learners. Our tools are technically sound to the maximum extent available.

- ☐ We approach the creation of a student-centered master schedule by considering time, people, and spaces as variables we can alter to impact changes in student outcomes.

- ☐ We are committed to working with the master schedule in a dynamic manner, meaning that we make adjustments based on student data and a clear understanding of our design, needs, current reality, and strengths.

- ☐ Our resulting master schedule reflects our beliefs, attitudes, values, and priorities.

- ☐ We are prepared to continuously improve our system, reflecting on the data, available resources, shared and our share values.

- ☐ We understand the value of social-emotional learning as a mechanism for building equitable support.

- [ ] We commit to regularly revisit our thinking around equity as we learn more about the historical pain of many and the incredible pride and individual humanity of each child and his or her family.

- [ ] We commit to learning the names of all our students, our coworkers, and their families.

- [ ] We celebrate all the family structures that make up our student and school population.

- [ ] We recognize that equity demands that we do more, even though we have already given so much.

- [ ] We recognize that throughout our careers we must challenge ourselves to deeply understand the students who come to us, and we commit to changing our practices as part of the way we do business.

- [ ] We work in a place where we know we have a voice, we belong, and we work daily to show others belong too.

- [ ] We see evidence of authentic student and family voice in our school community.

- [ ] We recognize and commit to MTSS as the framework for building equity in our school, and we support the time investment it will require over a number of years.

- [ ] We recognize that, no matter how long we have been working on equity, in many ways we are still just beginning.

- [ ] We recognize that we are educators, and we are quite simply amazing. ☺

Source: SWIFT Education Center (2016).

REFERENCES

Archer, A., Gleason, M., & Vachon, V. (2000). *REWARDS (Reading excellence: Word attack and rate development strategies)*. Longmont, CO: Sopris West Educational Services, Inc.

Batsche, G., Elliott, J., Graden, J. L., Grimes, J., Kovaleski, J. F., Prasse, D., … & Tilly III, W. D. (2005). *Response to intervention: Policy considerations and implementation.* Alexandria, VA: National Association of State Directors of Special Education.

CAST. (2018). *Universal Design for Learning Guidelines version 2.2.* Retrieved from http://udlguidelines.cast.org

Chuck Knox. (n.d.). BrainyQuote.com. Retrieved July 9, 2019, from https://www.brainyquote .com/quotes/chuck_knox_404662

Cloke, K., & Heckman, B. (2018). *Words of wisdom: Profound, poignant & provocative quotes.* Retrieved from https://www.amazon.com/Words-Wisdom-Profound-Poignant-Provocative/dp/1732704619

Council of Chief State School Officers & CEEDAR Center. (2015). *Promises to keep: Transforming educator preparation to better serve a diverse range of learners.* Washington, DC: CCSSO. Retrieved from http://ceedar.education.ufl.edu/wp-content/uploads/2015/06/Promises-to-Keep.pdf

Edmonds, R. (1979). Effective schools for the urban poor. *Educational Leadership, 37*(1), 15–24.

Espin, C. A., McMaster, K. L., Rose, S., Wayman, M. M. (2012). *A measure of success: The influence of curriculum-based measurement on education.* Minneapolis: University of Minnesota Press.

Hicks, T., McCart, A., & Choi, J. H. (2018, April). *Exploring the relationship between MTSS and inclusion: Bayesian fixed effects analysis.* Presentation at the American Educational Research Association Annual Meeting, New York.

Jackson, J. (2013). *Get a backbone, principal: 5 conversations every school leader must have right now!* Denver, CO: Outskirts Press.

Knight, J. (2014). *Creating learning partnerships: The principles behind instructional coaching.* Retrieved from www.instructionalcoach.org

Kramarczuk Voulgarides, C., Fergus, E., & King Thorius, K. A. (2017). Pursuing equity: disproportionality in special education and the reframing of technical solutions to address systemic inequities. *Review of Research in Education, 41*(1), 61–87.

Lane, K. L., Oakes, W. P., & Menzies, H. M. (2019). Comprehensive, integrated, three-tiered (CI3T) models of prevention: The role of systematic screening to inform instruction. In P. C. Pullen & M. J. Kennedy (Eds.), *Handbook of response to intervention and multi-tiered systems of support* (ch. 5). New York: Routledge.

McCart, A. B., McSheehan, M., Sailor, W., Mitchiner, M., & Quirk, C. (2016). *SWIFT differentiated technical assistance.* (White paper). Lawrence, KS: SWIFT Center.

McIntosh, K., & Goodman, S. (2016). *Integrated multi-tiered systems of support: Blending RTI and PBIS.* New York: Guilford Press.

Mijares, A., Montes, E., Hukkanen, S., & McCart, A. (2017, October 26). *All means all: Equity and access for all students through an MTSS framework.* Presentation at College Board Forum 2017, New York.

National Association of Secondary School Principals. (2011, May). *The master schedule: A culture indicator.* AP Insight Archives. Retrieved from https://authorzilla.com/DW8BZ/the-master-schedule-a-culture-indicator-nassp-national.html

Pullen, P. C., & Kennedy, M. J. (2019). *Handbook of response to intervention and multi-tiered systems of support.* New York: Routledge.

Sailor, W. (2009). *Making RTI work: How smart schools are reforming education through schoolwide response-to-intervention.* San Francisco: Jossey-Bass.

Sailor, W., McCart, A. B., & Choi, J. H. (2018). Reconceptualizing inclusive education through multi-tiered system of support. *Inclusion, 6*(1), 2–18.

Smolkowski, K., Girvan, E. J., McIntosh, K., Nese, R. N., & Horner, R. H. (2016). Vulnerable decision points for disproportionate office discipline referrals: Comparisons of discipline for African American and White elementary school students. *Behavioral Disorders, 41*(4), 178–195.

Sugai, G., Horner, R. H., & Gresham, F. (2002). Behaviorally effective school environments. In M. R. Shinn, H. M. Walker, & G. Stoner (Eds.), *Interventions for academic and behavior problems II: Preventative and remedial approaches* (pp. 315–350). Bethesda, MD: National Association of School Psychologists.

Swenson, S., Horner, R., Bradley, R., & Calkins, C. (2017, January 18). In recognition of Hill Walker's contributions to Multi-Tiered System of Supports (MTSS). [Blog post]. Office of Special Education and Rehabilitative Services. Retrieved from https://sites.ed.gov/osers/tag/hill-walker/

University of Texas Center for Reading & Language Arts. (2003, 2004). *3-tier reading model: Reducing reading difficulties for kindergarten through third grade students.* Austin: University of Texas System, Texas Education Agency.

U.S. Department of Education. (2014). *Practices to promote grade-level reading by third grade: My brother's keeper promising practices series* (vol. 1). Washington, DC: Author. Retrieved from https://www2.ed.gov/about/inits/ed/earlyliteracy/k-3-literacy-multi-tiered-systems-of-support.pdf

Van Norman, E. R., Nelson, P. M., & Klingbeil, D. A. (2017). Single measure and gated screening approaches for identifying students at-risk for academic problems: Implications for sensitivity and specificity. *School Psychology Quarterly, 32*(3), 405.

Wellman, B., & Lipton, L. (2000). Navigation. *Journal of Staff Development, 21*(1), 47–50.

INDEX

A SAGE Publishing Company

Helping educators make the greatest impact

CORWIN HAS ONE MISSION: to enhance education through intentional professional learning.

We build long-term relationships with our authors, educators, clients, and associations who partner with us to develop and continuously improve the best evidence-based practices that establish and support lifelong learning.

Solutions YOU WANT | Experts YOU TRUST | Results YOU NEED

EVENTS

>>> **INSTITUTES**

Corwin Institutes provide large regional events where educators collaborate with peers and learn from industry experts. Prepare to be recharged and motivated!

corwin.com/institutes

ON-SITE PD

>>> **ON-SITE PROFESSIONAL LEARNING**

Corwin on-site PD is delivered through high-energy keynotes, practical workshops, and custom coaching services designed to support knowledge development and implementation.

corwin.com/pd

>>> **PROFESSIONAL DEVELOPMENT RESOURCE CENTER**

The PD Resource Center provides school and district PD facilitators with the tools and resources needed to deliver effective PD.

corwin.com/pdrc

ONLINE

>>> **ADVANCE**

Designed for K–12 teachers, Advance offers a range of online learning options that can qualify for graduate-level credit and apply toward license renewal.

corwin.com/advance

Contact a PD Advisor at (800) 831-6640 or visit www.corwin.com for more information